D1295937

TRADING WITH CHINA

TRADING WITH CHINA

J. MARK MOBIUS
&
GERHARD F. SIMMEL

New York

Published 1973 by Arco Publishing Company, Inc.
219 Park Avenue South, New York, N.Y. 10003

Copyright © 1972 by Interasia Publications Ltd.

Library of Congress Catalog Card Number 72-92901
ISBN 0-668-02908-0

Printed in the United States of America

Map of Eastern China
with major cities

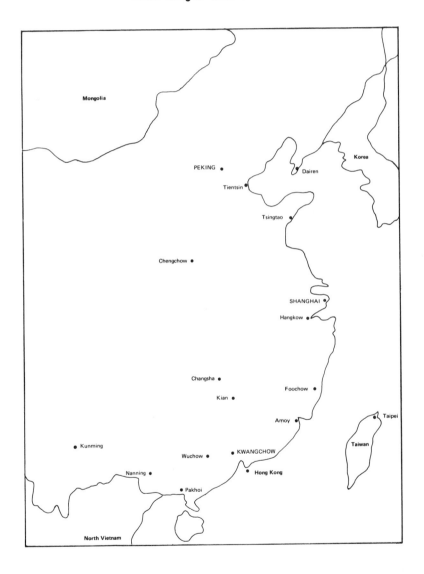

Contents

I. INTRODUCTION

The events of the past years, during which the People's Republic of China has become ever more integrated into the world's family of nations, have made businessmen of many nations increasingly aware of and interested in the possibilities of expanded trade with the giant of Asia, where an estimated 800 million people live in the third largest country of the world. Many countries have been involved in China trade for years, but the procedures for this trade have kept the foreign businessman very much at arm's length, without his ever having a chance to deal directly with Chinese producers or consumers. This is not new.

The first Middle Eastern and European traders to reach China over the 'Silk Route' two thousand years ago were required to keep their caravans at a distance from Chinese settlements and outside the walls of Chinese cities. Only a designated few citizens of the Middle Kingdom were permitted to do business with the foreigners, and popular contact with them was strictly forbidden.

In more modern times, at the beginning of the eighteenth century, European and American merchants who came over the sea routes to China were permitted to settle on a tiny, isolated isthmus called Macao jutting out into the South China Sea from the Pearl River delta. Periodically, they were permitted to sail up the river to their so-called 'factories' on a small strip of land outside the walls of Canton, to trade tea, and silk, and other products, but only through a group of special imperial merchants, or agents.

During the past decade, an increasing number of selected foreign businessmen have again been permitted to come to Canton (now called Kwangchow by the Chinese) twice each year to trade through a group of agents known as the State Trading Corporations of the People's Republic of China.

As a result of these limited trade encounters and conditions, there are many misconceptions about the potential, as well as the practices, of foreign trade with China. In view of her political and economic policies, the wishful thought of selling all types of consumer goods to 800 million potential Chinese customers is quite unrealistic; and, all too often, foreign entrepreneurs forget that China, like any other country, is also highly interested in selling her own products and commodities to foreign markets.

There is a very definite market in the People's Republic of China for goods and materials which she can only obtain from foreign sources, and which she needs to further her own industrialization, develop her own resources, and fill the basic needs of her ever growing population. At the same time, China has interesting and desirable export commodities, and is producing greater quantities and varieties of marketable products as her internal development progresses. However, expansion of this potential will take time.

In 1971, China's gross national product was only one-tenth that of the United States, while her population is almost four times that of the American industrial giant. Her per capita gross national product in 1971 was only equivalent to US$131, while it was in excess of US$5,000 in the United States. China's two-way foreign trade reached US$4.5 billion in 1971. This gives a per capita foreign trade of US$5.60 for China, while that of the United States is approximately US$380 per person, and Australia's as much as US$800 per person. China's gross national product has been growing at an estimated 4.5 per cent during recent years. Her current efforts at faster industrialization and development can increase this sharply in the near future. Her population, despite birth control, continues to grow by some 18 million persons each year. There is no question that her foreign trade must increase during the coming years.

The purpose of this book is to provide information for the foreign businessman, economist, or scholar into the background, trends and mechanics of trade with China, as well as to give some practical guidance to Chinese trading practices and the actual procedures of doing business with the People's Republic of China. Parts of the book can be used for reference, while other parts will give more background and insight into the complicated trading philosophy of the country.

Our information has come from many sources, and our sincere thanks go to the many businessmen from East and West, to the trade commissioners and consular trade officials representing their countries in Hong Kong, to the members of the China Resources Company and the Chinese General Chamber of Commerce, and to many veteran China traders who gave us so willingly of their time, their knowledge, and their experiences.

This book is not, nor can it be, complete. Conditions, policies, requirements, and practices of the People's Republic of China will continue to change as they have done in the past. But the trend is toward increased commerce, and we believe and hope that this book will be informative and useful for the foreigner interested in this expanding China trade.

II. THE HISTORY OF CHINA TRADE

EARLY FOREIGN CONTACTS

The real beginnings of China's international trade are difficult to delineate since, throughout its history, Chinese hegemony extended to a number of surrounding countries. It might be said that China's international influence and exchange started during the Han Dynasty (206 B.C. to A.D. 220) when China's power extended as far as Annam (Vietnam), Korea, and the Caspian Sea. At one time the Han Chinese even encountered the Roman Legionnaires in battle. Roman artifacts indicate that the Romans had access to goods from China. Contacts with the outside world at that time included the sending of valuable gifts of Chinese goods to the 'barbarians' in surrounding countries to keep them peaceful.

During the Tang Dynasty (A.D. 618 to A.D. 906) there were extensive dealings with foreigners. Foreign missionaries of many faiths, including Nestorian Christians, propagated their religions while Moslem merchants plied their trade. Foreigners were employed in the Tang government and foreign imported goods were used in daily life. Tang influence extended to Turkestan and even penetrated into India.

CHINESE DOMINANCE IN ORIENT TRADE

The Sung Dynasty (A.D. 960 to A.D. 1279) was marked by the establishment of government business enterprises and state monopolies. The development of shipping and navigation during this time resulted in Chinese control of maritime commerce in the Orient, previously dominated by the Arabs. This was the time when Marco Polo arrived in China. Polo was in Hangchow, the capital of the Sung when the Mongols arrived. The stories he told upon his return to Europe in 1292 stirred the imagination and interest of European traders.

Mongols overthrew the Sung Dynasty and established the Yuan Dynasty, the first non-Chinese regime to control all of China. The surge of national consciousness and xenophobia resulting from the discrimination against native Chinese by the ruling Mongols helped in the downfall of the Yuan and establishment of the Ming Dynasty (1364 to 1644). At the zenith of Ming power, Chinese ships sailed as far as the east coast of Africa. The exchange of tributes and gifts between China and the nations of Asia reached a large enough volume at this time to constitute international trade.

11

EUROPEANS REACH CHINA BY SEA

During Ming rule the Portuguese were the first Europeans to discover a sea passage to China, and as early as 1517 the Portuguese were trading there. In 1557 they obtained permission from the Ming emperor to settle in what is now known as Macao. They thus enjoyed the monopoly of the trade in Europe of those commodities which the Chinese were willing to sell them. After 1580, when Portugal became part of Spain, the Spanish started using Macao as a terminal port in their trade between Mexico and Manila.

The British were the third European nation on the scene when, in 1625, Captain Weddell landed in Macao. However, despite the flourishing development of British-Indian trade conducted by the East India Company monopoly, the British were unsuccessful in opening China trade during the 1600s.

EARLY EXPANSION OF TRADE WITH THE WEST

In 1644 the Manchus overthrew the Ming Dynasty and established the Ch'ing Dynasty which ruled China until 1911. The consolidation and strengthening of Ch'ing power was primarily carried out by Emperor K'ang-hsi (1654-1722) and his grandson Ch'ien-lung (1711-1799). Their reigns were marked by the reassertion of Chinese dominance over Mongolia and Turkestan, the checking of Russian expansion in the far north, and the invasion of Tibet, Nepal and Bhutan.

Since Emperor K'ang-hsi had a curiosity and taste for foreign ideas, he allowed Jesuits to live and work in his capital. But as a result of this contact he learned to distrust them after discovering their plans to undermine the Confucian system. Nevertheless, he saw the value of deriving income from trade with the west and, in 1685, opened ports to the Europeans. Soon after, however, he restricted such trading to Canton only and governed it by the 'Eight Regulations' which bear careful study since they reflect the sensitivities shown by the Chinese to this day. In essence the 'Regulations': (1) provided an area [called the 'factories' (warehouses)] in Canton where the foreign merchants (without their families) were allowed to live and carry on business only during the winter shipping season from September to March, (2) restricted arms and armed vessels, (3) required the licensing of pilots, boatmen and agents working for the foreigners, (4) limited the number of servants allowed, (5) prohibited sedan chairs and boating for pleasure as well as (with some exceptions) excursions into the city or its neighborhood, (6) restricted trade through Chinese 'hong' merchants selected by the Government to do all business with the foreigners and receive all complaints and petitions, (7) prohibited smuggling and credit, and (8) restricted trading ships to Whampoa (thirteen miles below Canton) for loading and unloading.

By the time Emperor Ch'ien-lung died in 1799, Britain had emerged as the leading military power in Europe with dominance over such powers as Portugal and Spain. This growth in power was reflected in the British East India Company's predominance over China trade. However, sharing the 'factories' at

Canton at the turn of the century were the Danish, Dutch, Spanish, French, Swedish and Americans.

Early trade between the Europeans and Americans and the Chinese consisted primarily of Chinese exports of silk and tea balanced by imports of cotton goods and furs. However, there was a persistent trade imbalance in China's favor with the necessity of the European traders having to make up the balance in silver bullion. However, the East India Company was soon able to redress this situation by replacing silver with opium, the export of which the Company also monopolized in India.

Despite the banning of opium imports by the Chinese Government, the trade continued to expand with the East India Company selling to private traders who, in turn, expanded smuggling activities along the China coast.

Europe and China Clash

By the 1830s official exports from China to Britain and other countries totalled about US$5 million with about US$3 million transacted by British firms, a little less than US$2 million by American firms and the small remainder by the other European firms (mainly from Holland and France). However, the illegal opium traffic was at least three times that of the official trade. Total legal and illegal trade was therefore about US$20 million per year with a balancing US$20 million in imports for a total of US$40 million.

In 1834 the East India Company lost its monopoly over trade with China. The result was a rapid growth of private firms, led by Jardine Matheson. By this time, China was suffering from a graft-ridden and inept government following a rigid Confucian system. The population pressure of 300 million was resulting in less land per capita and increasing shortages of food. The entry of a strong Britain on the scene followed by other Western nations desiring to trade coincided with the rise of local rebellions, secret societies and antimonarchical movements. The meeting of East and West at this time revealed a scene where the Chinese government arrogantly regarded the Europeans as barbarians, thus scorning their desire for expanded trade, while the Europeans looked down on the Chinese as backward and decadent. This situation combined with the Chinese Emperor's determination to end opium smuggling (despite collusion in the smuggling by Chinese officials) resulted in the first war ever waged between China and the West since Roman times. The results of this were the Treaty of Nanking in 1842, which forced the Chinese to cede the island of Hong Kong to England, the legalization of opium traffic, and the granting of diplomatic equality and commercial privileges to British subjects. These privileges were soon extended to the Americans and other nations. Balking by the Chinese at infringements on their sovereignty resulted in the seizure of Peking and the burning of the Summer Palace in 1844 by British and French forces. This pattern of extracting additional concessions by force was followed by foreign powers until Europeans essentially controlled Chinese economic life.

Between the Treaty of Nanking in 1842 and the Treaty of Shimonoseki in

1895, no less than eighteen foreign countries extracted from the Chinese Government a broad range of trading privileges. Foreigners were therefore able to enjoy extra-territorial rights, be exempt from Chinese taxation, live and trade in their own concessions and settlements, pay low import duties, avoid internal taxes on imports and exports, have their ships sail Chinese coastal and inland waters, and even have administrative control of the Customs and Post Office.

TRADE IN THE EARLY 1900s

In 1911, the Ch'ing Government was overthrown and the Republic of China was established. The years following were marked by futile attempts to establish a parliamentarian form of government. China entered World War I in 1917 and was able to regain some territory lost to the Japanese. After the Washington Conference in 1922, President Sun Yat-sen started a series of military operations to unify the country and defeat the warlords who controlled various provinces. During these years a semblance of order was obtained in China. Tariff autonomy was achieved, and some foreign nations were persuaded to surrender their extra-territorial rights. However, in 1931 Japan invaded Manchuria starting the major war which was to destroy China's economy.

Before 1930, Chinese trade with the West was mainly conducted by European and American merchants. It was not until after 1930 that Chinese firms began to do business on a large scale and the Chinese Government started to purchase direct from Western producers. This pattern was also true of trade financing, with foreign banks having control up until the 1930s.

In 1931 foreign investment in China was estimated to be US$2.5 billion dollars. (The equivalent today would be approximately US$6.8 billion.) Of this total, the U.K. held 37 per cent, Japan 35 per cent, and the U.S. and France 6 per cent each, with other nations holding smaller shares. The pattern and composition of trade changed drastically in the early 1900s. In the latter part of the previous century, one-third of all imports consisted of opium and one-third of cotton, while exports mainly consisted of tea (46 per cent) and silk (34 per cent). However, by 1929, although cotton goods still constituted the largest single category of imports, the reduction of the opium trade was replaced by trade in cereals, sugar, fuel, chemicals and metals. With increasing local production of cotton goods and yarn in addition to domestic cotton cultivation, cotton raw materials and finished goods imports had a continuous decline while imports of chemicals and metals increased. By 1936 iron, steel and metal imports were the largest import category followed by chemicals and dyes, liquid fuel and kerosene, machinery and transport materials.

Composition of China's Imports

1925		1936*	
Item	Per cent share	Item	Per cent share
Cotton goods	16	Iron and steel, metals	13
Sugar	10	Chemicals and dyes	11
Liquid fuel and kerosene	8	Liquid fuel and kerosene	8
Raw cotton	7	Machinery	6
Cereals	7	Transport materials	6
Chemicals and dyes	6	Cereals	4
Iron and steel, metals	5	Raw cotton	4
Cotton yarn	4	Sugar	2
Transport materials	2	Cotton goods	2
Machinery	2	Wheat flour	1
Wheat flour	2	Others	43
Others	31		
TOTAL	100	TOTAL	100

* Excluding Manchuria which
was under Japanese control.

While during the late 1800s Chinese exports consisted mainly of tea and silk, by 1925 beans and bean cake predominated over tea although silk and silk goods remained the leading Chinese export with 23 per cent of total exports. By 1936, seeds and oils from seeds were the leading export with 19 per cent of the total while tea exports had declined to 4 per cent. Export growth during the 1925 to 1936 period was shown in eggs, hides, leather, ores and metals, and cotton goods. Other exports included such items as bristles, feathers, and tung oil.

Composition of China's Exports

1925		1936	
Item	Per cent share	Item	Per cent share
Silk and silk goods	23	Seeds and seed oil	19
Beans and bean cake	16	Silk and silk goods	8
Seeds and seed oil	8	Ores and metals	8
Cotton and cotton goods	6	Cotton and cotton goods	7
Eggs and egg products	4	Eggs and egg products	6
Tea	3	Hides, leather, skins	6
Ores and metals	3	Tea	4
Coal	3	Coal	2
Others	34	Beans and bean cake	1
		Others	39
TOTAL	100	TOTAL	100

Before World War II, Chinese exports were of poor quality due to lack of government standards and control in addition to the problem of small scale manufacturing. In 1936 a Bureau of Testing and Inspection was established but by that time the silk trade had, to a great extent, been lost to Japan.

In 1919, Japan, with 31 per cent of all of China's imports, was the major supplier to China followed by Hong Kong and the United States. By 1936, the U.S., with 20 per cent of China's imports, had emerged as the major supplier, followed by Japan and Germany.

China's Major Suppliers

1919		1936	
Country	Per cent of total imports	Country	Per cent of total imports
Japan	36	U.S.A.	20
Hong Kong	23	Japan	16
U.S.A.	16	Germany	16
U.K.	9	U.K.	12
France	5	France	2
Others	11	Hong Kong	2
		Others	32
TOTAL	100	TOTAL	100

THE WAR YEARS

Between 1937 and 1945 China's economy was in great confusion because of the war. The immediate postwar years were marked by tremendous inflation. Foreign aid was the main support at that time. In the four years following the Pacific War, total foreign aid was estimated to have been US$2.25 billion, mostly supplied by the U.S. During those immediate postwar years exports were large because it was again possible to move the enormous stocks of raw materials which had accumulated. Between 1946 and 1948 total yearly imports averaged US$552 million while yearly exports averaged US$178 million. The result of the imbalance was a rapid fall of gold and foreign exchange assets.

The U.S. was China's leading trading partner during the postwar period supplying an average of 62 per cent of China's imports and taking an average of 27 per cent of China's exports in the 1946 to 1948 period. During that time, Hong Kong led the U.S. as the largest buyer of Chinese products.

China's Major Suppliers, 1946 to 1948

Country	Per cent of total imports
U.S.	62
Hong Kong	19
U.K.	7
India	7
Southeast Asia	4
Others	1
TOTAL	100

China's Major Buyers, 1946 to 1948

Country	Per cent of total exports
Hong Kong	31
U.S.	27
Southeast Asia	12
U.K.	5
India	4
Others	21
TOTAL	100

By 1948, the condition of China's economy was desperate despite U.S. aid. The People's Liberation Army expanded its drive to control China. At the end of 1949 the new government was formed and the Nationalist government fled to Taiwan. In June of 1950 war between North and South Korea broke out. By December, President Truman had announced a ban on all American ships and aircraft trading with Communist China and a similar ban on the loading or unloading of cargo to any point in the world if there was reason to believe that any of the goods were destined directly or indirectly for Communist China. All Communist Chinese assets within American jurisdiction were frozen.

III. RECENT CHINA TRADE TRENDS

KOREAN WAR PERIOD

The Korean War, which lasted from 1950 to 1953, marked the first years of the Communist's administration of China. During those war years, the Chinese government consolidated administrative control of the country. From a low point of approximately US$1.4 billion in 1950, China's total trade increased steadily even during that period so that by the end of the war total trade had reached about US$2.2 billion.

FIRST FIVE YEAR PLAN

About the time of the Korean truce in 1953, major political reorganization was begun, in addition to the introduction of the First Five Year Plan. The Plan lasted from 1953 to 1957. In 1954 the National People's Congress elected Mao Tse-tung the First Chairman of the People's Republic of China and Chou En-lai the Prime Minister. As implementation of the Plan progressed, the process of agricultural collectivization accelerated along with nationalization of industrial facilities. By the end of the Plan in 1957, private enterprises in China had practically been eliminated. Total trade during the Plan period rose from US$2.2 billion in 1953 to US$3.0 billion in 1957.

THE 'GREAT LEAP FORWARD'

The Second Five Year Plan lasted from 1958 to 1962 and was marked by a dramatic increase in trade followed by a sharp decrease. In 1958, the first year of the 'Great Leap Forward', total trade increased to US$3.8 billion, an increase of US$800 million from the US$3.0 billion 1957 figure. Again in 1959 total trade made another jump as a result of greatly increased trade with Russia, and the figure reached US$4.6 billion, the highest point in the 1950 to 1971 period. The excesses of the 'Great Leap Forward' with its inefficient 'backyard furnaces' and organizational problems in the commune movement were reflected in the 1959 to 1962 period of 'post-leap decline'. This was compounded by the Sino-Soviet rift and the withdrawal of Soviet assistance. During that period, trade dropped from the 1959 high of US$4.6 billion to a low of US$2.7 billion in 1962. Because of the drop in industrial and agricultural output, food stockpiles were depleted and China embarked on large scale imports of wheat. An intensive program to raise agricultural output was begun with concomitant needs in the fertilizer and farm equipment areas.

THE 'GREAT LEAP' RECOVERY

The period between 1963 and 1965 was one of recovery for China's economy, so that overall production rose to the same level it had reached immediately preceding the 'Great Leap Forward'. During this recovery period, total trade showed a steady increase so that by 1966 it had reached a high of US$4.2 billion.

CULTURAL REVOLUTION AND RECOVERY

Between 1966 and 1968 the economy was threatened again. The beginning of the Cultural Revolution resulted in disrupted agricultural and industrial production. Most critical was the interruption of transportation facilities which hampered the proper distribution of goods. Total trade declined in 1967 to US$3.7 billion and stayed static at almost the same level until 1970 when the increases in agricultural production and general recovery of the economy from the Cultural Revolution were reflected in an increase of total trade to an estimated US$4.3 billion. The latest figures available for 1971 indicate a further increase to approximately US$4.5 billion.

BROAD TRADE TRENDS

Looking at the broad trend of China trade during the twenty-one year period from 1950 to 1970, China's total trade, including imports and exports, never exceeded US$4.6 billion. That peak of US$4.6 billion was reached in 1959. The lowest yearly figure was found in 1950 when total trade was US$1.4 billion. However, despite the relatively low level of Mainland China's trade, (Taiwan's trade in 1970 was US$2.9 and US$4.2 billion in 1971), the long term trend has been upward although there were intervening years of wars and political upheavals. Our short and long-range statistical straight-line projections from 1950 and 1960, respectively, show parallel upward trend lines with total trade estimated for 1980 at between US$5.3 and US$5.7 billion. This is a conservative projection and takes into consideration all the downward movements in the last twenty years. With recent political events, a more optimistic projection would certainly not be out of the question.

TRADE BALANCE

China's trade balance between 1950 and 1955 was negative with yearly imports exceeding exports by between US$62 and US$214 million. However, in the years between 1956 and 1969, China's trade balance was favorable with excesses of exports over imports ranging between US$32 million and US$428 million. In 1970, for the first time in 14 years, China's trade sank into a deficit position.

Projections from a long-term view starting in 1950 show that China's trade balance will be positive and that eventually China will be exporting much more

20

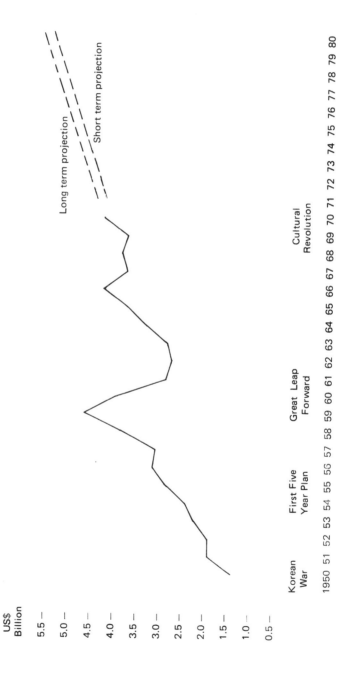

China total trade – 1950 to 1970

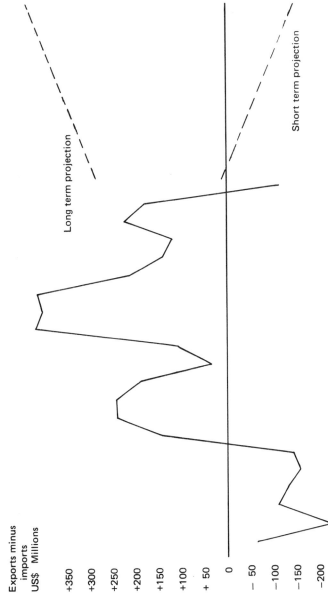

China's trade balance — 1950 to 1970

Exports minus imports US$ Millions

Long term projection

Short term projection

+350
+300
+250
+200
+150
+100
+ 50
0
− 50
−100
−150
−200

1950 51 52 53 54 55 56 57 58 59 60 61 62 63 64 65 66 67 68 69 70 71 72 73 74 75 76 77 78 79 80

21

than it imports. However, taking the short-term projection from 1960, the trend is definitely toward a deficit picture with China's imports exceeding exports. China needs capital equipment and infrastructure in order to build its export industries to the point where they can compete on world markets in both soft and hard goods. Once the capital building and infrastructure task is completed, China will probably become a supplier of consumer and industrial goods far surpassing the scale of Japan.

COMMUNIST BLOC TRADE

The percentage of China's total trade with Communist bloc countries has shown a decreasing trend since 1954. Between 1950 and 1955 the percentage of China's total trade with the Communist bloc increased from 29 per cent to 74 per cent of all trade. However, from that time, the yearly percentage of Communist bloc trade to total trade decreased, recovered slightly in 1959, and then steadily decreased so that by 1970 only 20 per cent of China's trade was with the Communist bloc. The long-term projections from 1950 show a continuation of this decreasing trend.

It seems that there is almost a direct correlation between China's increasing volume of trade and the decreasing share of participation by the Communist bloc. Between 1951 and 1962 over 50 per cent of China's trade was with the Communist bloc. During those years ideological factors were, of course, important. However, more important were the restrictions by the West on trade after China's entry into the Korean War. After 1959 the failure of the 'Great Leap Forward' and the subsequent depression combined with the effects of the Sino-Soviet dispute caused the total volume of trade to fall sharply. Between 1966 and 1968, the Cultural Revolution did not help to boost external trade figures.

LEADING TRADING PARTNERS

China's leading trading partners in recent years have included Japan, Hong Kong, West Germany, Australia, the United Kingdom, Canada, France, Singapore, Italy and Malaysia. Japan, China's leading trading partner in 1970, with 20 per cent of China's total trade, exported double the amount she imported from China. Japanese exports have included industrial merchandise such as steel products, heavy-duty trucks, machines and parts, machine tools, and chemical fertilizers. Chinese exports to Japan have mainly been in the area of agricultural products such as oilseeds, silk and other raw materials.

Hong Kong is China's second leading trading partner and the largest market for China's exports besides being the major source of her foreign exchange. In 1970 China's exports to Hong Kong were US$354 million while imports from Hong Kong were only US$5 million. In addition to direct imports from China, Hong Kong imports a number of goods for re-export. This, added to remittances and business earnings of Chinese enterprises in Hong Kong, added up to a total of US$625 million gross income for China earned in Hong Kong during 1970. In

Percentage of China's Total Trade with Communist Countries —
1950 to 1970

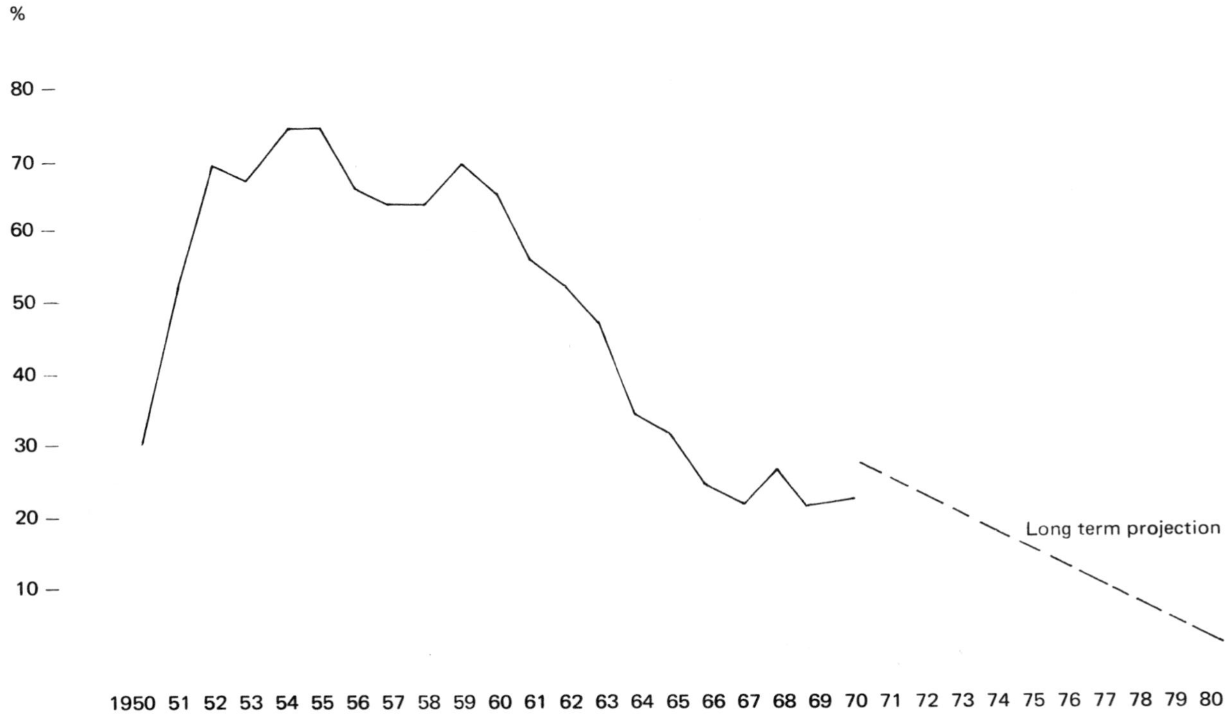

Long term projection

80 −

70 −

60 −

50 −

40 −

30 −

20 −

10 −

%

1950 51 52 53 54 55 56 57 58 59 60 61 62 63 64 65 66 67 68 69 70 71 72 73 74 75 76 77 78 79 80

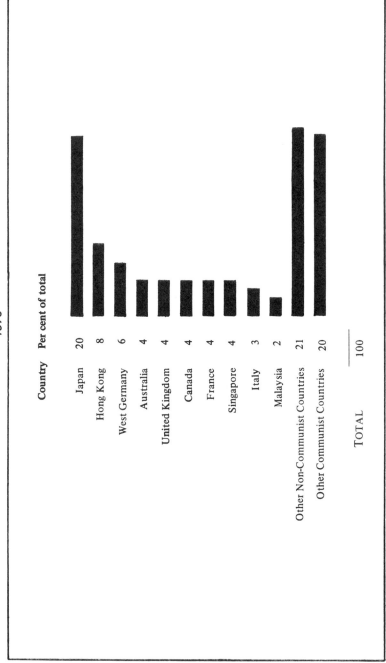

China's Total Trade by Country
1970

Country	Per cent of total
Japan	20
Hong Kong	8
West Germany	6
Australia	4
United Kingdom	4
Canada	4
France	4
Singapore	4
Italy	3
Malaysia	2
Other Non-Communist Countries	21
Other Communist Countries	20
TOTAL	100

1971 this figure grew to something in the neighborhood of US$700 million. China's exports to Hong Kong alone grew from the 1970 figure of $354 million to $550 million in 1971. (This 1971 figure is based on the value of the U.S. dollar prior to devaluation which took place in the fall of 1971.)

CHINA'S LEADING TRADE PRODUCTS

In recent years the main exports of China have been foodstuffs, textiles and clothing. In 1970, 48 per cent of all China's exports consisted of foodstuffs while 22 per cent consisted of textiles and 15 per cent clothing. Leading buyers of all these commodities have been Hong Kong and Japan. Major imports have included machinery and equipment, iron and steel, wheat and chemical fertilizers. In 1970, 24 per cent of all imports consisted of machinery and equipment while 21 per cent consisted of iron and steel, 19 per cent wheat, 11 per cent chemical fertilizers and 10 per cent rubber. Japan has been a leading supplier of iron and steel, machinery and equipment and chemical fertilizers, with the U.K., West Germany and other European countries as additional top suppliers. Australia, Canada and France have been leaders in the supply of wheat while Singapore, Malaysia and Ceylon have been the primary rubber suppliers.

China's major imports

Item	1970 per cent of total imports	Leading suppliers
Wheat	19	Australia, Canada, France
Iron and steel	21	Japan, West Germany
Machinery and Equipment	24	Japan
Rubber	10	Singapore, Malaysia, Ceylon
Chemical fertilizers	11	Japan
Other	8	Japan
TOTAL	100	

China's major exports

Item	1970 per cent of total exports	Leading buyers
Foodstuffs	48	Hong Kong, Japan
Textiles	22	Hong Kong, Japan
Clothing	15	Hong Kong, Japan
Other	15	Hong Kong, Japan
TOTAL	100	

IV.   WHAT CHINA BUYS AND SELLS

Trading with China is not a private matter between producer and consumer, directly, or through agents, distributors or representatives. All imports and exports are handled through specific State Trading Corporations. They are fully responsible for all negotiation on specifications, prices, conditions, deliveries, terms of payment and so forth, on behalf of the Chinese producers or consumers.

The State Trading Corporations are the official purchasing and selling agents for the People's Republic of China. Each handles a specific group of products, both for import and for export. Their main offices are in Peking, but they also have branch offices throughout the country in various locations, depending on the specific products involved.

It is with these seven State Trading Corporations that direct contact should be made to initiate commerce with China. They are listed at the end of this chapter, together with their addresses, branches, and the products or commodities which each one is handling.

Main Chinese Imports

China's import requirements have varied greatly in the past, depending on internal conditions and production as well as on the changes in economic philosophy and goals of the Communist Chinese leadership.

While about one-third of China's imports during the late 1950s consisted of machinery and equipment, foodstuffs were only about two per cent of the total imports during these years. The situation changed drastically following the twin disasters of the 'Great Leap Forward' and adverse weather conditions, when farm output dropped radically at the end of that decade.

In the early 1960s, foodstuffs suddenly made up as much as 40 per cent of the country's imports, while machinery imports dropped to less than 10 per cent of the total.

Since 1965, despite the temporary industrial disruptions of the Cultural Revolution, China's economy has been going steadily upward, both in industrial and agricultural production. However, she has had to continue imports of grain to supplement her own production, and wheat continues to be one of her prime purchases. Chemical fertilizers and pesticides are also constant requirements and are imported in large quantities.

All kinds of machinery and equipment — agricultural, industrial, technical, electrical and otherwise — as well as whole industrial plants and foreign technical know-how are now needed by China in order to further her mechanization and more thoroughly develop her own sources of raw materials. Major amounts of transport machinery, including locomotives, trucks, cargo ships, and airplanes have also been purchased in recent years.

Although China's own iron and steel production is increasing rapidly, additional amounts of these as well as a variety of steel products are another major import item. A variety of other raw materials, chemicals and ores are required for her industries.

During 1970, China spent an estimated US$360 million on machinery and equipment, US$315 million on iron and steel imports, US$290 million on wheat, US$170 million on chemical fertilizers, and US$110 million on non-ferrous metals in her import program.

MAIN CHINESE EXPORTS

Basically an agricultural country, China has traditionally exported large amounts of foodstuffs, even during the difficult years of the early 1960s. Although she needs to buy wheat, China is the world's third largest exporter of rice; the higher-priced rice earns much of the foreign exchange needed to pay for the wheat. Early in 1972, China reduced her export price of rice twice within weeks in an apparent attempt to find more buyers and increase the revenues earned with this commodity. A wide range of other foodstuffs is exported by China. Major items include meat and meat products, fruits and vegetables and tea.

Textiles and clothing have become increasingly important exports as additional mechanization has permitted China to increase her production. About one-third of her total recent exports consists of textile fibers, products and clothing. China also sells a large variety of crude animal and vegetable materials, minerals, edible oils and, in recent years, an increasing selection of consumer goods from sporting articles to household goods and transistor radios.

China exports in order to pay for her imports; she tailors her export commodities and prices to her import needs.

COMMODITY LISTING

For easy reference, import and export commodities are listed below according to their Standard International Trade Classifications (SITC) and sectors. The E/I designation before each item indicates whether the commodity is primarily exported or imported by China, or both.

Letter designations at the end of each item specify the State Trading Corporation(s) responsible for that particular commodity, as listed at the end of this chapter. These trading corporations are responsible for both export and import.

FOOD AND LIVE ANIMALS

00 – E –   *Live animals.* About 1,000 head of cattle and 4,000 hogs daily were exported to Hong Kong in 1971 to earn over US$95 million for China. China is now seeking to import some animals for breeding purposes and has shown interest in Canadian stock. (F)

01 – E –   *Meat and meat preparations* are exported by China in major amounts, primarily to Hong Kong (US$37.5 million in 1971), but also to Japan, Germany, England, France and Egypt. (A)

02 – E –   Some *dairy products* are exported, primarily to Hong Kong. (A)

03 – E –   *Fish and fish preparations* are exported to Hong Kong (US$38 million in 1971) and, in smaller amounts, to Australia, Japan and other countries. (A)

04 – I/E –   *Cereals.* China imported almost five million metric tons of wheat in 1970, but less in 1971. It is still one of her major imports. Canada became the prime supplier of this commodity after she formally recognized the People's Republic, replacing Australia which had been the main source previously, but which does not have diplomatic relations with China. China exports large amounts of rice to Ceylon, Malaysia, North Vietnam, Pakistan, the Philippines, Hong Kong, England, Cuba and various Arab and African countries. (A)

05 – E –   A large variety of *fruit* and *vegetables,* both fresh and dried, are exported to Hong Kong, Canada, Australia, England, Germany, Holland, Singapore, Japan and others. Exports to Hong Kong totalled more than US$56 million in 1971. (A and F)

06 – E/I –   China has been importing *sugar* from Cuba, Guyana and Peru to supplement her own production. She has also approached Brazil and Mexico for additional supplies due to Cuban crop failures in 1971. At the same time, China has indicated that she is prepared to export refined sugar to Malaysia in order to obtain some raw materials from that country. China is also the world's third largest exporter of *honey,* which is generally more 'flowery' than that of other producers. (A)

07 – E/I –   *Tea and spices* are a major export to Australia, Canada, England, Hong Kong and other countries. Some *coffee* is imported from Peru. (F)

08 – E –   *Animal foodstuffs* are exported to Japan and Hong Kong. (F)

BEVERAGES AND TOBACCO

11 – E –   *Beverages,* especially Chinese wines, are exported to Hong Kong,

Singapore and other countries with large Chinese populations. (A)

12 – E/I – China is importing small amounts of *tobacco* from Greece. At the same time, she exports her own tobacco to Germany and has offered it to Japan. (F)

CRUDE MATERIALS

21 – E/I – *Hides and skins* are exported to a number of countries including Australia, Canada, England, Italy and Japan. China also imports some lamb skins from Australia. (F)

22 – E – *Oil seeds, nuts and kernels* are a major Chinese export item, especially to Japan, Hong Kong and Italy, but also to many other countries. Foreign requests for these products are usually much larger than supply. (A and F)

23 – I – *Crude rubber* is a major import from Singapore, Malaysia and Ceylon. Over 150,000 tons annually have been imported by China in recent years, but 1971 orders were less than in previous years. Synthetic and rubber substitutes are also of interest to China. (B)

24 – I – *Wood and timber* are imported by China from Malaysia and Africa, and she has expressed an interest in Canadian lumber. (F)

25 – I – *Pulp and waste paper.* Pulp is imported from Finland and other Scandinavian countries, and China is looking to Canada for additional supplies. (C)

26 – E/I – *Textile fibers.* China is one of the world's major sources of raw silk, with large amounts exported to Italy, Japan, Germany, England and many other countries. At the same time, cotton, wool, and an increasing amount of synthetic fibers are imported from Australia, England, France, Italy and Japan. (G)

27 – E – *Crude fertilizers and crude minerals* are sold to Australia and England. (B)

28 – I/E – *Metalliferous ores and scrap* are a major trade item. Aluminum, zinc, lead, tin, and iron ore and scrap are all in heavy demand even though China has vast deposits of some of these. To fill her needs, she makes major purchases from Australia, Canada, Britain, Germany, Japan, Zambia and others. At the same time, China is also a major producer of antimony, mercury, magnesium and tungsten, and exports them to Japan and Europe. (E).

29 – E – *Crude animal and vegetable materials* include hog bristles and duck feathers, two of China's largest export commodities, of which US$13 million were sold to England alone in 1971. Major additional amounts went to Japan, Germany, Australia and,

indirectly, even to the United States. (A and F)

MINERALS AND LUBRICANTS

32 – E – *Coal,* both bituminous and anthracitic, is found in good supply in China. Minor quantities have been exported to Japan and other Asian countries. (E)

33 – I/E – *Petroleum and petroleum products.* Although it is estimated that China has at least 50 years' supply of petroleum and claims to be self-sufficient in this field, specialized products are imported from Albania, Egypt, Iraq and Rumania. China is also obtaining technical know-how in petroleum production from the latter two countries, and is seeking additional refining plants and technical aid from Japan. China may start exporting petroleum products within the next few years. (B)

ANIMAL AND VEGETABLE OILS AND FATS

4 – E/I – A variety of these items are exported to Hong Kong, Japan and other trading partners. At the same time, China has expressed interest in importing more tallow. (A)

CHEMICALS

51 – I/E – *Chemical elements and compounds,* both organic and inorganic are purchased by China in great amounts, particularly from Japan and Germany, but also from England and other countries. Among China's requirements are hydrocarbons and their derivatives, alcohols, phenols, inorganic esters, salts, acids and halogenated derivatives. Some specific chemical elements are exported by China to Japan, England and other countries. (B)

53 – I – *Dyeing, tanning, and coloring materials* are purchased in Europe by China. She needs synthetic organic dyestuffs, natural indigo, color pigments, color lakes, paints, varnishes and related materials to supplement her own production. (B)

54 – I/E – Some amounts of *medical and pharmaceutical products* are imported from Europe and Japan, and China has additional requirements in this field, although much of her medicine still relies on natural remedies. Chinese herbs and medicines are exported to Asian countries. (B and F)

55 – E – Small, but important, amounts of *essential oils* are sold by China to many countries. (F)

56 – I – China's need for *manufactured fertilizers* far outstrips her own production, and she purchases about 60 per cent of Japan's total

production. Additionally, she imports this item from Chile, Italy, Norway, Germany, among others. (B)

57 – E – *Explosives and pyrotechnic products.* China exports fireworks to Australia, Japan, Singapore and other countries, primarily in Asia. (C)

58 – I – *Plastics and cellulose* are purchased by China from England, Finland, Italy and Japan. (B)

59 – I/E – *Chemical materials and products* are imported from a number of European countries. Insecticides, fungicides, and disinfectants are a major need, and imports come primarily from Japan. China also exports some chemical products. (B)

MANUFACTURED GOODS AND METALS

61 – E – *Leather manufactures* are exported to Japan and Europe. (C)

64 – I/E – *Paper and paperboard* are imported by China from Scandinavia, and China is seeking paper-making technology. Paper products are exported, primarily through Hong Kong. (C)

65 – E/I – *Textile yarns, fabrics and made-up articles* are one of China's main exports. Large amounts are sold to Japan, Germany, England and Hong Kong, while smaller amounts go to almost every one of China's trading partners. At the same time, China needs to import additional cotton yarn, synthetic fiber yarns, woven fabrics of wool, animal hair, and man-made fibers. (G)

66 – E/I – *Non-metallic mineral manufactures,* especially housewares and tableware, are a major export item for China, with large amounts going to Japan, Europe, Singapore and Hong Kong. At the same time, China needs to import glass and glass articles and a variety of precious and semi-precious (industrial) stones. Fifteen per cent of China's total 1971 trade exchange with England fell into this category. (E)

67 – I – *Iron and steel* is purchased by China in large amounts since her own production falls far short of her increasing needs. More than two million metric tons have been purchased from Germany and Japan recently, with additional purchases from Algeria, Austria, Canada, Romania, Sweden and the United Kingdom. China needs pig and cast iron, bars, rods, angles, shapes, sections, universal plates, sheets, strip, tubes, pipes and fittings. (E)

68 – I/E – *Non-ferrous metal,* especially copper, is purchased by China in major quantities from various sources of supply in Europe, Africa

31

and South America to supplement her own production. China also seeks lead and lead alloys, zinc and zinc alloys, nickel, unwrought aluminum, aluminum and copper alloys and products Despite her own needs, China exports such products to smaller countries. (E)

69 – I/E – *Metal manufactures* are imported by China from Japan and Eastern and Western Europe. These include hand tools, blowtorches, anvils, vices, clamps, machine tools and spares, power-operated hand tools, base metal electrodes, wire and rods. China also exports her own metal products, primarily to Asian and African countries. (E)

MACHINERY AND TRANSPORT EQUIPMENT

71 – I/E – *Machinery (non-electric)* is one of China's prime needs: Germany provided large amounts of tool machinery in 1971, and additional agricultural machinery, construction machinery and office machinery is being purchased from Eastern and Western Europe as well as Japan. A large consignment of jet engines was purchased from England early in 1972. Other items sought by China are steam generating boilers, machines for loading and hauling, compressors, all types of pumps, and specialized machinery for textile and paper-making. China is exporting light machinery to Asian and African countries. (D)

72 – I/E – *Electrical machinery* is imported by China primarily from England, Germany and Japan. Generators, motors, converters, transformers, rectifiers, switching apparatus, X-ray equipment, telecommunications and measuring equipment, as well as computers are of prime interest to China. *Electrical appliances* are not being imported. Instead China is beginning to export such items of her own manufacture and is seeking a wider market for these in Asia, Africa and South America. (C and D)

73 – I – *Transport equipment* is another major need in China, and she has purchased large numbers of railway locomotives in recent years. She has also purchased large numbers of trucks from European countries and Japan. Several Japanese automobile manufacturers are considering the sale of whole motor vehicle assembly plants to China. Purchases of, and interest in further purchases of, commercial airplanes have increased in recent months, with negotiations under way by major plane manufacturers following purchases from England and the Soviet Union. China has bought a large number of cargo ships in recent years and, to supplement her own shipbuilding capabilities, has given orders to Japan and Yugoslavia. (D)

MISCELLANEOUS MANUFACTURED MATERIALS

81 – I/E – Some high quality *fixtures and fittings* for plumbing, heating and lighting are being sought and imported by China, while she herself exports lower quality products of this type to Asian and African countries. (D and E)

82 – E – Common, as well as traditional Chinese, *furniture* is exported through Hong Kong and Singapore. (C)

83 – E – *Travel goods* are exported primarily to Asia, but some luggage is also sold to Eastern and Western Europe. (C)

84 – E – One of China's main export items, *clothing* is sold to almost all trading partners led by Japan and Hong Kong. Clothing exports exceeded US$200 million in 1970. (G)

85 – E – *Footwear* is exported by China to Asian and European markets, and Chinese manufacturers have shown a willingness to custom manufacture from samples. (F)

86 – I/E – *Professional, scientific and control equipment* is required by China in great variety and amounts and is imported from Japan, Switzerland, Germany, England and Eastern Europe. Photographic goods, as well as clocks and watches, are being produced in China and sold to neighboring Asian countries and Canada. Traders feel that Chinese cameras will soon compete with Japanese products in quality and price. (D)

87 – E – *Miscellaneous manufactured articles,* especially household and sporting goods, toys and artistic handicrafts are another major export item, primarily through Hong Kong and Singapore, but also directly to Japan, England and other trading partners. (C)

As is very evident, a full range of commodities is involved in China trade. Although some items may not be imported or exported at any particular time, a change of conditions or economic planning in China can affect import needs or export availability very quickly. The above listing is not complete. Non-mention of any product does not mean that there may not be a market for it, or a supply which might be purchased.

It may be noted that, in some cases, China will import a commodity of which she is a producer herself and may be exporting the same item to another area.

Although China has large natural resources, their limited development, and the major problems of transportation and distribution often make import necessary or more practical. In some cases also, China imports commodities not for her own needs, but to supply them as foreign aid to less developed nations.

The People's Republic of China is showing increasing interest in the purchase of complete plants and know-how from foreign countries. Recent imports of this kind include a polyethelene plant and a gas turbine power plant from England, and a synthetic textile fiber plant from Japan. China is also considering the purchase of motor vehicle assembly plants and petroleum refining technology during 1972. (D)

THE STATE TRADING CORPORATIONS OF CHINA

(A) CHINA NATIONAL CEREALS OILS AND FOODSTUFFS IMPORT AND EXPORT CORPORATION,
82 Tung An Men Street
Peking, People's Republic of China
Cable Address: CEROILFOOD PEKING

Branches in: Peking, Nanning, Tientsin, Kian, Dairen, Kunming, Foochow, Chengchow, Hankow, Shanghai (2), Changsha, Kwangchow and Tsingtao (2).

Imports and exports: Cereals, edible vegetable and animal oils and fats, vegetable and animal fats for industrial use, oil seeds, seeds, oil cakes, feeding stuffs, salt, edible livestock and poultry, meat and meat products, egg and egg products, fresh fruit and fruit products, aquatic and marine products, canned goods of various kinds, sugar, sweets, wines, liquors and spirits, dairy products, vegetables and condiments, bean flour noodles, grain products, nuts and dried vegetables, etc.

Hong Kong agents:

(Cereals and Oils)   China Resources Co.
Bank of China Building
2A Des Voeux Road
Hong Kong, B.C.C.
Cable Address: CIRECO HONGKONG

(Foodstuffs)   Ng Fung Hong Co.
Bank of China Building
2A Des Voeux Road
Hong Kong, B.C.C.
Cable Address: NGFUNG HONGKONG

(B) CHINA NATIONAL CHEMICALS IMPORT AND EXPORT CORPORATION
Erh Li Kou
Hsi Chiao
Peking, People's Republic of China
Cable Address: SINOCHEM PEKING

Branches in: Shanghai, Tientsin, Kwangchow, Tsingtao and Dairen.

Imports and exports: Rubber, rubber tires and other rubber products; petroleum and petroleum products; chemical fertilizers, insecticides and fungicides; pharmaceuticals, medical apparatus, instruments and supplies; chemical raw materials, dyestuffs, pigments, paints, printing inks, etc.

Hong Kong agent: China Resources Co.
Bank of China Building
2A Des Voeux Road
Hong Kong, B.C.C.
Cable Address: CIRECO HONGKONG

(C) CHINA NATIONAL LIGHT INDUSTRIAL PRODUCTS IMPORT AND EXPORT CORPORATION
82 Tung An Men Street
Peking, People's Republic of China
Cable Address: PROCHINA PEKING

Branches in: Peking (3), Shanghai (2), Tientsin (2), Kwangchow (2), Dairen, Tsingtao, Foochow (2), Changsha, Hankow and Nanning.

Imports and exports: Paper and boards, general merchandise, stationery, musical instruments, sporting goods, toys, educational supplies, building materials and electrical appliances, radio and television sets, photographic equipment and supplies, fish nets, net yarns, leather shoes, leather products, pottery and porcelain, human hair, pearls, precious stones and jewelry, jade carvings, lacquerware, plaited articles, furniture, artistic and other handicrafts, etc.

35

Hong Kong agent: Hua Yuan Company
37 Connaught Road West
Hong Kong, B.C.C.
Cable Address: GYCOMP HONGKONG

(D) CHINA NATIONAL MACHINERY IMPORT AND EXPORT CORPORATION
Erh Li Kou
Hsi Chiao
Peking, People's Republic of China
Cable Address: MACHIMPEX PEKING

Branches in: Shanghai, Tientsin, Kwangchow, Tsingtao and Dairen.

Imports and exports: Machine tools, presses, hammers, shears, forging machines, diesel engines, gasoline engines, steam turbines, boilers, mining machinery, metallurgical machinery, compressors and pumps, lifts, elevators and hoists, winches and cranes, transport machinery and motor vehicles (and parts), vessels and marine equipment, agricultural machinery and implements, printing machines, textile machines, knitting machines, building machinery, rubber and plastic-making machines, machines for other light industry, tools, ball and roller bearings, electric machinery and equipment, telecommunications equipment, electronic and electric measuring equipment, scientific instruments, meteorological, geological and optical instruments, complete industrial plants, technical expertise, etc.

Hong Kong agent: China Resources Co.
Bank of China Building
2A Des Voeux Road
Hong Kong, B.C.C.
Cable Address: CIRECO HONGKONG

(E) CHINA NATIONAL METAL AND MINERALS IMPORT AND EXPORT CORPORATION
Erh Li Kou
Hsi Chiao
Peking, People's Republic of China
Cable Address: MINMETALS PEKING

Branches in: Shanghai, Tientsin, Kwangchow, Dairen, Tsingtao, Nanning, Foochow and Kunming.

Imports and exports: Steel plates, sheets and pipes, sections, tubes and special steel; railway materials; metallic products; pig iron, ferro-alloys, non-ferrous metals, precious rare metals, antimony, tin, mercury, tungsten ore, non-metallic minerals and products; coal, borax, cement, hardware, etc.

Hong Kong agent: China Resources Co.
Bank of China Building
2A Des Voeux Road
Hong Kong, B.C.C.
Cable Address: CIRECO HONGKONG

(F) CHINA NATIONAL NATIVE PRODUCE AND ANIMAL BY-PRODUCTS IMPORT AND EXPORT CORPORATION
82 Tung An Men Street
Peking, People's Republic of China
Cable Address: CHINATEX PEKING

Branches in: Peking, Kwangchow (4), Shanghai (3), Fukien, Amoy, Tientsin (2), Hankow, Kunming, Changsha, Dairen, Tsingtao (2), Nanning, Wuchow and Pakhoi.

Imports and exports: Tea, coffee, cocoa, tobacco, bast fiber, rosin, feeding stuffs, timber, forest products, spices, essential oils, nuts and dried vegetables, patent medicines and medicinal herbs, bristles, horse tails, feathers, down, white rabbit hair, wools, cashmere, camel wool, yak hair, casings, brushes, skins and hides, leathers, fur mattresses, fur products, carpets, down products, live animals, etc. Also dressed hair tails, fine hairs, goat hair, bedding feathers, bones, horn and hoofs, etc.

Hong Kong agent: Teck Soon Hong, Ltd.
37-39 Connaught Road West
Hong Kong, B.C.C.
Cable Address: STILLON HONGKONG

(G) CHINA NATIONAL TEXTILES IMPORT AND EXPORT CORPORATION
82 Tung An Men Street
Peking, People's Republic of China
Cable Address: INDUSTRY PEKING

Branches in: Peking, Shanghai (2), Tientsin, Tsingtao, Kwangchow (2) and Dairen.

Imports and exports: Synthetic fibers, fiber fabrics, raw cotton, raw wool, cotton cloth, cotton yarn, raw silk, silk filament yarns, silk articles and ready-made garments, cotton piecegoods, woollen piecegoods, knitwear, blankets, towellings, artificial fibers, knitted piecegoods, linen, garments and wearing apparel, tablecloths, drawn work and embroidery.

Hong Kong Agent: China Resources Co.
Bank of China Building
2A Des Voeux Road
Hong Kong, B.C.C.
Cable Address: CIRECO HONGKONG

37

V. TRADE MECHANICS

Since the foreign trader has almost no chance at all of ever making direct contact with the end consumer or the original supplier of any goods in China, a knowledge of the internal economic procedures which initiate foreign trade is necessary and helpful.

GOVERNMENT IMPORT AND EXPORT STRUCTURE

China's trading plans can be divided into three parts: (1) long-range, which are part of the five year plans; (2) annual, which are formulated during the latter half of the preceding year; and (3) quarterly, which are derived from the annual plans and the necessary changes therein due to fluctuations in conditions or requirements. In the past, these plans have been formulated by the State Planning Commission, which sets up targets or quotas for the Chinese economy on the basis of Communist Party directives and the data supplied by the State Statistical Bureau.

If an agricultural commune in Anhwei province, for example, needs 20 tractors, the request would be forwarded via regional and provincial offices to both the Ministry of Agriculture and the State Planning Commission.

The Ministry of Agriculture would have to weigh the request with those from other communes, determine the availability of tractors from internal sources either through domestic manufacture or through a shift of supply, and consider the production goals of the particular agricultural sector involved. Possibly, this one request would be combined with others from communes throughout the country, and a total need of, say, 800 tractors would be determined. This would be forwarded to the State Planning Commission together with other long-term, annual, or quarterly requirements by the Ministry of Agriculture.

If the import of tractors is approved in principle by the State Planning Commission, the request is forwarded to the Ministry of Foreign Trade, which will ask the appropriate State Trading Corporation for information regarding specifications, availability, delivery time and competitive prices on the world market for the required tractors. This study is returned to the Foreign Trade Ministry to enable them to include a specific item of 800 tractors (of certain specifications and price) in their listing of proposed imports, which are sent to the State Council and the National People's Congress for approval.

When this approval has been obtained, the State Trading Corporation concerned is given the order to locate and purchase the required tractors at the best possible price and conditions.

A similar procedure prevails for the export of Chinese commodities. The State Planning Commission has statistical information on all internal production and requirements, and allocates amounts of foreign exchange to be earned by various sectors of the economy.

If a foreign customer wants to purchase from China an item which has not already been approved or made available for export, the request comes through the State Trading Corporation in question to the Ministry of Foreign Trade, which asks the State Planning Commission to study the feasibility of making such an export. Even if the particular commodity is not in surplus or normally available for export, the decision to export might be made (and production quotas or internal consumption adjusted accordingly) for political reasons or, more often, to earn foreign exchange to pay for more vital imports.

The availability of any export item is always limited, and foreign customers are seldom able to obtain the requested amount of any item. In some cases, a previously available item will suddenly no longer be available to a foreign purchaser. This can have a variety of causes besides true lack of supply or production: the need to fill the order of another country which has more important products required by China; political, business, or personal dissatisfaction with the customer or his country; or just plain business leverage to persuade the customer to buy some less desirable items in order to obtain a supply of the desired one.

This also explains why prices for Chinese goods sometimes change quite unpredictably. In addition to the above factors, prices also depend on the amount of foreign exchange which each industrial or commodity sector has been budgeted to earn.

China continues to aim for balanced trade, with exports paying for all imports. The basic principle remains as stated in 1954: 'Export is for import, and import is for the country's socialist industrialization.' This philosophy, coupled with China's aim to be self-sufficient in all areas, means that goods of interest to the People's Republic of China are limited. While the idea of a potential market of 800 million people is a highly tempting one, the chances of selling basic or luxury consumer goods to China are very slim in the near future. A realistic determination of the suitability of any product for the Chinese market must be made with these factors in mind.

MAKING CONTACT

Once the foreign businessman is convinced that his product is of possible interest to China and, where necessary, the export license for the product from his own country will be granted, the first approach can be made to the particular State Trading Corporation concerned with this commodity. (See listings in chapter IV.)

This first contact is very important for all future relations. It should consist of a letter signed by a leading official of the company stating the desire to

The 'long march' between China's producers or consumers and the foreign traders

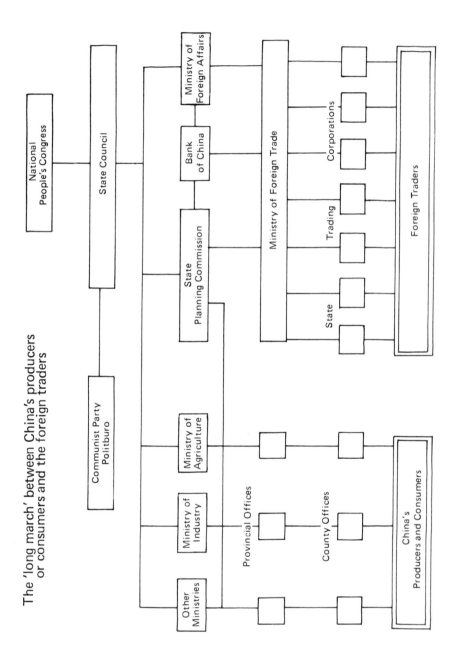

introduce a product in the hope that the People's Republic of China will find it useful. The letter will have attachments describing the product in detail, but it should also offer to provide more information and samples, and indicate availability for direct discussions if the Chinese are interested.

To this letter should be attached, first of all, detailed information about the company and its activities. This should be comprehensive, giving information about the history of the company and its top officials, as well as its business activities and involvements. It is important that the presentation be accurate and candid, since China has excellent sources on world business and can check the given information.

Secondly, very detailed information about the product being offered should be given, including full specifications and descriptions as well as informative pamphlets, pictures and diagrams. Dimensions, weights, etc. should be given in metric units. Emphasis must be placed on providing information rather than making a sales pitch, since the latter is liable to have the opposite effect in dealings with the People's Republic of China. While general information on availability and delivery times should be included, most experienced traders feel that prices should not be quoted in the initial approach.

All this information should be sent in at least six copies, although ten or more copies are preferred. Where the commodity concerned is handled by two trading corporations, approaches to both should be made, since they may not exchange information. Since all the State Trading Corporations have varying numbers of branches, it would be wise to send information in sufficient quantities to permit copies to be sent to all of them, and also to provide some to competent industrial experts for assessment of the product.

Correspondence should be in English. Having descriptions, pamphlets and other information about the product translated into Chinese is of doubtful value for the initial contact. It is also rather difficult, since they would have to be translated into the modern simplified Chinese characters used in the People's Republic of China.

Airmail from the United States to China takes about one week, but it will take many weeks or months before the State Trading Corporation will have a chance to process the letter and the information. Considering the great number of products handled by each of the trading corporations, and the great number of offers and requests they must consider both from within China and from all over the world, the immensity of their job can well be imagined.

The fact that months may pass without any response can mean that they are studying the product and offer in great detail. Or, it can mean that they are not interested.

SAMPLES AND QUOTATIONS

If the Chinese are interested, a request for additional information, specifications, performance data, samples and prices will be forthcoming, and should be answered in all possible detail. Samples should not be sent unless they have been requested or approved. Then, unless other instructions are given, they should be sent to the Hong Kong representative of the State Trading Corporation concerned, and he will forward them.

Price quotations should be in detail and straightforward. The Chinese know world markets extremely well and seek the most competitive prices. Quotations should be FOB at a European or American West Coast (probably Canadian) port where Chinese or Chinese-chartered ships call regularly.

The quotations should be in a currency acceptable to the People's Republic of China. The U.S. Dollar has not been in this category in the past, but business was done in U.S. Dollar quotations at the 1972 Spring fair in Kwangchow. Quotations in British Pound Sterling have been best in the past, since the Chinese are used to dealing in this currency and their own currency, the Renminbi, has had a stable relationship with the pound. For commercial purposes, the Bank of China has pegged the Renminbi to the Swiss Franc, quoting a cross-rate of 1 yuan to 0.563 Swiss Francs.

Lately, the People's Republic of China has been insisting on writing all import contracts in Renminbi, payable in Peking, but correspondent banks of the Bank of China will handle the conversion of the Renminbi to foreign currencies for a slight charge.

Purchasing Goods

In order to buy Chinese products, the procedures are basically the same. An approach should be made to the State Trading Corporation concerned by letter, giving details of the foreign company and indicating a desire to purchase certain commodities. Specifications, weights, amounts, and any other requirements should be stated in great detail.

Although the People's Republic of China has tended to sell commodities on a 'take-it-or-leave-it' basis in the past, some changes have been noted by China traders recently. They do want to sell, and they are making greater efforts to satisfy customer requests. Labelling of foodstuffs or other items can be done in English or several other languages as requested; special manufactures or packaging to customer wishes are also beginning to be considered, with the foreign purchaser being asked to supply samples to be copied. Specifically, this has been done in the areas of footwear, handbags, housewares and packaging.

Multiple copies of correspondence for purchase of Chinese commodities are, of course, less necessary, but many traders do enclose two copies with the original letter to the State Trading Corporation. Samples will not usually be provided by the Chinese State Trading Corporations except during negotiations at their bi-annual export commodities fair. Prices, when quoted, will be CIF to ports called on by Chinese or Chinese-chartered ships or, in some cases, CIF to Hong Kong, where the customer will need to arrange for onward shipment.

Continuing Negotiations

Although communication will become easier once a specific interest in customers or products is shown by the Chinese State Trading Corporation, considerable time will still pass between contacts. It must be remembered that the trading corporation must act as a clearing house in relaying requests for information and the given answers between the producer and the consumer — and this takes time.

In some cases, the State Trading Corporation in Peking may ask that further correspondence and negotiation be done directly with one of their branches, specifically interested in, or concerned with, the product involved. However, unless so instructed, all correspondence should be with the Peking head office only.

Letters should be addressed to the State Trading Corporation, and not to any individual therein, even if all return correspondence is signed by the same official. Even more important is that mail be properly addressed to 'The People's Republic of China.' It should never be addressed to 'Communist China', 'Red China', or 'Mainland China', since any indication that there might be 'another' China will cause the mail to be delayed, and probably refused, by the postal authorities of the People's Republic of China.

In this respect, mention of any past or present representation, trade or business associations with Taiwan, or the Republic of China (Nationalist) should be avoided in any correspondence, literature or negotiations with the People's Republic of China. One hopeful Western businessman, whose product had elicited considerable interest from the Chinese State Trading Corporation, suddenly received a curt letter from Peking terminating the negotiations after his secretary had inadvertently enclosed a brochure mentioning the company branch address in Taipei in a mailing to the State Trading Corporation.

As negotiations continue by mail, the Chinese State Trading Corporation may invite the foreign businessman or his organization to come to the Kwangchow (Canton) Export Commodities Fair, or to come to Peking for further discussions. It would also be advisable for the foreign trader to express interest in such a visit in his letters, since almost no contracts are ever finalized without face-to-face meetings with the State Trading Corporation officials in China.

Of course, there may not be any response at all to the initial approach, or only a brief note advising that no current need of an offered product, or availability of a desired commodity, exists. This should not end the matter. Experienced traders advise that up-to-date information on specifications and improvements in products, especially ones which will make the product more interesting to the Chinese, should be sent periodically. Similarly, interest in the purchase of Chinese products should be expressed by repeated letters.

Reference to previous correspondence should be made wherever warranted, but it would be well for any product information or specifications to be complete in each letter, thus eliminating the need to refer to previous correspondence. The State Trading Corporation will not systematically check through its voluminous files, and chances for success are better when it does not have to do so. Where a foreign businessman is in a position to both buy from and sell to China, this should be mentioned in correspondence, although individual contacts on sales and purchases must be made, especially when different State Trading Corporations are involved.

ALTERNATIVE APPROACHES

In some cases, an overseas subsidiary rather than the corporate headquarters may be in a better position to initiate contact with China. Especially in countries with diplomatic relations with Peking, or where Chinese trade offices or delegations are present, opportunities for contact may present themselves. In these cases, the Chinese officials will forward information from prospective suppliers or customers to the State Trading Corporations in Peking. In a few instances, overseas Chinese commercial offices have represented the State Trading Corporations in negotiations for a specific item. Occasionally, Chinese officials in overseas locations have been known to make the initial contact to a supplier when the product involved was of particular interest or need to the Chinese.

The Hong Kong representatives of the Chinese State Trading Corporations, especially the China Resources Company, operate as agents for these corporations, and have been authorized to negotiate, buy and sell commodities in specific instances. They are a continuing contact point for information, and are in constant communication with the State Trading Corporations in Peking. Business representatives visiting the area can call on these Hong Kong representatives to obtain information on China's commodity requirements and availability, and forward through them information about products or interest in purchases. This is a way to establish contact, although the State Trading Corporations prefer to deal directly with foreign firms.

National industrial exhibitions in China, when permitted, are another ideal way to present foreign products to the People's Republic of China. The first of these was held by Denmark in early 1972, and a number of European countries, as well as Canada, will be showing their products in Peking during the year. China will certainly utilize these foreign exhibits to make new contacts and negotiate for desired items. The possibility of participating or having a foreign subsidiary participate should be closely investigated.

In some cases, approaches through a third party may be most effective in initiating trade with China. There are a number of large and experienced China trading firms in Hong Kong. Many of these are European, with long-established commercial relationships with the People's Republic of China and the State Trading Corporations. Working through them has the obvious advantage of having an intermediary who knows the procedures of China trade and is already known to the Chinese. They may also be able to better utilize their 'equality and mutual benefit' philosophy of two-way trade by selling goods to China for one client while purchasing an equivalent amount of other goods from China for another client. Working through a third party will, of course, add a commission to the transaction cost.

There is considerable debate among China traders as to whether a third party approach will, in fact, be more successful than a direct one, once the political decision to trade has been made by China and the foreign businessman's country. In more than one case, successful Hong Kong traders have been unable to get an offer from China for an export commodity for a third party while, at the same time, a direct approach has received an immediate response.

If all else fails, or no advance contacts have been made, an invitation to the bi-annual export commodities fair might be obtained through a direct approach to: THE SECRETARY, CHINESE EXPORT COMMODITIES FAIR, PEARL RIVER SQUARE, KWANGCHOW, PEOPLE'S REPUBLIC OF CHINA. Such a letter should again include the information suggested in the initial approach to the State Trading Corporations, together with a request for an invitation to the fair.

This approach cannot be made at the last minute. It should be made at least three months in advance of the fair date, and it has been successful in the cases of a few Western businessmen whose countries have diplomatic or trade relations with the People's Republic.

In most cases, the initial contact will not find much response, and repeated offers over a period of time will be required for newcomers to enter the China market.

THE KWANGCHOW TRADE FAIR

The bi-annual Chinese Export Commodities Fair in the southern Chinese city of Kwangchow (Canton) is a major business event which attracts invited visitors from all over the world, and gives a unique opportunity for China traders to engage in practical business negotiations with China's State Trading Corporations.

The fair is held every year from April 15th to May 15th, and from October 15th to November 15th. Recently, they have been attended by as many as 20,000 visitors from dozens of countries, including thousands of overseas Chinese from neighboring Asian countries. Among foreign businessmen, the Japanese have been the largest group, with approximately 2,500 representatives from almost 1,000 firms coming to recent fairs. Other major contingents come from West Germany, Canada, Australia, Britain, France, Italy, Sweden and Norway, each of which had more than 100 businessmen attending the Kwangchow exhibition recently.

Since it is an export fair, it offers an excellent opportunity to study the latest range of Chinese products for purchase. However, since the same State Trading Corporations are involved in the import of goods into China, the fair is also used as a major venue for the Chinese to get in touch with businessmen having goods to sell to the People's Republic. Although foreign companies are beginning to have an opportunity to show their products in China through national industrial fairs in Peking, negotiation for as much as one-half of all China's foreign trade is done at Kwangchow. Business firms interested or engaged in trade with China should make a point of attending these fairs regularly.

The fair is located in a ten-story building connected to two adjacent halls on

Pearl River Square, only a short distance from the waterfront area where modern trade with China commenced one hundred and thirty years ago. The buildings house the fair administration as well as all the exhibitions, which are organized according to the products handled by each of the State Trading Corporations. Programs or plans of the fair are not published, and the novice trader will have to rely on help from veterans or from fair officials to find the location of the particular State Trading Corporation with which he wishes to do business.

The fair is normally open from 8.30 a.m. to 11.30 a.m., and from 2.00 p.m. until 5.30 p.m. on weekdays, but is closed on Saturday afternoons and Sundays. Admission is by a special badge, which is issued to the businessman on arrival and registration at his hotel.

Once the desired State Trading Corporation has been found, a Corporation official, who can be recognized by his badge, must be contacted. The foreign trader should introduce himself with his business card, on which his hotel and room number should be written. At this time, he should request an appointment to discuss business at the earliest possible opportunity. Depending on the crush of other traders, such an appointment could take place immediately, but newcomers find that it usually takes one or several days.

Appointments cannot be made in advance from outside China, so veteran traders usually rush over to the fair immediately after their arrival in Kwangchow in the afternoon to arrange for a first business session on the following morning. Newcomers will usually have to wait longer for their initial meeting, but this should not unduly discourage them. The very fact that an invitation to the fair has been issued indicates an interest on the Chinese side.

BUSINESS CONFERENCES

Negotiating sessions take place around tables at the side of the exhibition floors, or in private rooms available at the discretion of the Chinese officials. The foreign businessman should have his full file of previous correspondence available at these meetings. Also, when selling, he should have additional copies of the product literature for study by the State Trading Corporation officials. The State Trading Corporations assemble staff from all their branches to come to Kwangchow every half year, so the negotiators may not have had a chance to see this material previously. The Chinese State Trading Corporation will be represented by at least two, sometimes more, officials and an interpreter will also be present. Sometimes, other State Trading Corporation or Foreign Trade Ministry officials might also join in the discussions. Even though the Chinese officials may know and speak English, the actual negotiations will be carried on in Chinese through an interpreter.

Despite the many demands on the State Trading Corporation officials' time, the initial meeting will usually be very casual in order to become acquainted before actually getting down to business. While a Westerner might be impatient to end the pleasantries, this small talk is part of any business session in China and should not be undervalued. During and shortly after the Cultural

Revolution, foreign businessmen found themselves spending most of their time listening to expositions of Communist Chinese ideology and policies during these business discussions, but this has been almost totally eliminated in recent years.

The foreign businessman must be sensitive to matters of 'face'. Chinese officials will not normally discuss the need for specific foreign products, or admit that they may not be available from China's own production. The visitor is expected to want to serve the People's Republic with his products, rather than to emphasize his desire to sell and make money. During actual negotiations, the foreigner will find the Chinese extremely well informed about world markets and prices, and also of previous sales practices and the background of the foreigner's company. He will also find that they are very astute bargainers. As everywhere, quality and price are important factors in negotiations with the State Trading Corporations of the People's Republic of China, but there are others.

POLITICAL, ECONOMIC AND PERSONAL CONSIDERATIONS

Politics play a varying role in China's business practices. If the Chinese do not wish to trade with a particular country for political reasons, the trading organizations will not respond to approaches from that country, or issue invitations to the Kwangchow fair to businessmen of that country. Even when the approach is made in an indirect way, it will be ignored.

However, once contact has been established and once invited to Kwangchow, most foreign businessmen feel that the political factors become much less important. There seems good evidence for this view, since neither Japan, China's largest trading partner with US$899 million in two-way trade in 1971, nor Germany, her largest European trading partner with US$222 million in two-way trade in 1971, have diplomatic relations with the People's Republic of China. While their trade has been prospering, that of Great Britain, who was one of the first nations to recognize the People's Republic of China politically in January 1950, had been declining drastically for several years until early 1972 when Sino-British relations were finally raised to ambassadorial level.

On the other hand, China's aims at self-sufficiency, and her trade philosophy of 'equality and mutual benefit' do affect specific negotiations. Rather than rely on a supply of some particular item from only one producer or one country, China's State Trading Corporations will purchase smaller amounts of the same item or commodity from a number of different suppliers and countries. Similarly, China's efforts to maintain balanced trade with all countries will affect purchases and sales, and foreign businessmen must remember that they are not only viewed as traders in a specific commodity, but also as traders from a specific country — for economic rather than political reasons.

All this applies to negotiations for the purchase of Chinese goods. Buyers will seldom be permitted to buy the full amount requested of any item, since the Chinese prefer to spread the available supplies among many customers. However, while the Chinese State Trading Corporations will negotiate at length on the price and conditions of products purchased by them, there is little such negotiation on the Chinese products they sell. The price is set and so are the terms and conditions.

As with most people, the Chinese tend to give some preference to old acquaintances, such as trading partners with whom they have done business successfully in the past, possibly for many years. But the extent of this preference is quite limited when it comes to actual business. "I get my appointments more quickly, while the newcomers have to sit around and wait," says one trader, "and that's as far as my advantage goes."

On his first visit to Kwangchow, the foreign businessman may find that he will be quite indifferently received, has difficulty getting appointments, and must spend hours waiting for them. However, if he shows patience and politeness and handles himself well in his contacts with the Chinese, he can expect increasingly better receptions during subsequent visits.

Three to five business sessions are normally required to finalize negotiations, but they can also take much, much longer. Especially on the sale of products to China, negotiations can take weeks and require a visit to Peking, or even to Shanghai, after the fair, before the contracts are completed.

Since the Kwangchow fair is for export, the Chinese do give preference to selling their goods. Experienced businessmen say that the Chinese spend the first three weeks of the fair selling, and only the final weeks in buying. Traders coming to sell products to China must be prepared to spend a much longer time than buyers, and will find themselves waiting for appointments day after day. For newcomers, especially, the People's Republic of China places importance on attendance at the opening ceremonies on the first day of the Kwangchow Fair, even though no business can be accomplished on that day. This means that foreign businessmen must sometimes spend the full period of the fair in Kwangchow, even though no decisive or fruitful negotiations come about until the final week.

A successful purchase from, or sale to, China is no guarantee or indicator for future negotiations, nor will the trader ever be able to obtain information on future needs or availability of products from the State Trading Corporations.

Trade with China requires a great deal of patience, time and perseverance. Success also requires a sensitivity to Chinese customs and temperament, as well as an appreciation of their business etiquette and practices.

A European trader in Hong Kong puts it very bluntly: "Buying from China is difficult; selling to them is murder!"

The dimensions of the potential business make it worthwhile.

VI. VISITING CHINA

TRAVEL DETAILS AND DOCUMENTATION

Once an invitation to visit the People's Republic of China, especially to the Kwangchow (Canton) Trade Fair, has been issued by one of the State Trading Corporations, the issuance of a visa is usually a routine matter. First, however, the invitation comes with an acceptance form which should be returned as soon as possible. If for any reason it is impossible to accept the invitation, a letter advising this and expressing regrets should be written to avoid offending the Chinese hosts.

Application for a visa must be made at a diplomatic mission of the People's Republic of China (in Ottawa, London, Paris or Bern), or to an office of the China Travel Service. American businessmen have recently been told to make their applications through Ottawa, by writing to the EMBASSY OF THE PEOPLE'S REPUBLIC OF CHINA, 100 BRONSON AVENUE, OTTAWA, CANADA. For other nationalities, obtaining a visa through the CHINA TRAVEL SERVICE (HK) LTD., 37 QUEEN'S ROAD CENTRAL, HONG KONG, is usually most convenient since so many travellers to China do come via Hong Kong.

In either case, a photocopy of the invitation to come to China, or to the Kwangchow Fair, must be enclosed with the letter requesting the visa application forms. The completed forms must then be returned to the appropriate office which will arrange for the visa to be issued. If the visa is to be mailed, the traveller's passport as well as the original invitation card to China must be submitted with the completed visa application forms. Both will be returned with the visa, since the original invitation card is needed for presentation on arrival in China.

Those who make their application through the China Travel Service can arrange to pick their visa up personally in Hong Kong on their way to China, but this is not necessary. If the visa is not applied for until the traveller has already arrived in Hong Kong, he must expect a delay of some days before it is issued, especially during the busy time of the Kwangchow Fair. Once the traveller has obtained his visa and made his travel plans, China Travel Service will take care of all further details, including ticketing, hotel reservations, handling of baggage, interpreters and guides (where necessary) and any other requirements. They will also assist in any extensions or changes of visa, and in obtaining the necessary exit visa before the departure from China.

Prospective visitors should make sure that their passport is valid for the

People's Republic of China (some older U.S. passports have a restriction against China travel) and that the passport does not expire during the period of the China visit. They should also be aware that the People's Republic of China does not recognize the Nationalist Republic of China on Taiwan. Therefore, evidence of visas from the Nationalist authorities, or visits to Taiwan, should not appear in the passport. If necessary, a new passport should be obtained before applying for a visa to the People's Republic. All travellers to the People's Republic of China must have valid international certificates of vaccination against smallpox and cholera when arriving in China.

TRAVEL ROUTES TO CHINA

Direct air service into the People's Republic of China is very limited. In early 1972, only Air France, Pakistan International Airlines, and Russia's Aeroflot had weekly services from their respective capitals to China. Therefore, the routing via Hong Kong, which can be reached by numerous air or sea carriers from all parts of the world, is the most popular.

Kwangchow is only 90 miles north-west of Hong Kong. Visitors coming from Hong Kong take the train on the Kowloon side to the Chinese border, cross the Lo Wu railway bridge on foot, and then take a Chinese train to Kwangchow after completing the border formalities. The round-trip fare from Hong Kong to Kwangchow is approximately US$20, including possible meals in transit at the Chinese border. Luggage is normally checked through to the hotel in Kwangchow by the China Travel Service, but the traveller is expected to carry his own hand baggage across the bridge at Lo Wu, especially on the return trip from China.

When applying for a visa, it is important that the means of travel, the points of entry into and departure from China, and all areas to be visited are correctly and precisely stated, since delays and difficulties will result if these details are not correct in the visa.

HONG KONG TO KWANGCHOW

Normally, travellers to China take the train from Kowloon Station − across the harbor from Hong Kong island itself − at about 8.30 a.m. During the one hour trip to the Chinese border, they will fill out currency as well as customs declarations, detailing all moneys, personal effects, baggage and samples being carried. Rings, watches, pens, valuable cigarette lighters, photographic equipment, radios, tape recorders, liquor, cigarettes and other tobaccos, foodstuffs (instant coffee) and any other goods or valuables must be itemized.

There is usually no problem for visitors to bring into China reasonable amounts of any of the above items for personal use during the stay, but none of these items may be sold or given away while in China. *Bona fide* gifts of less than US$20 total value may be brought into China, but must be declared together with the name of the recipient. Discretion should therefore be used in the type of gifts carried to avoid complications for the recipient as well as for the traveller. Publications, phonograph records or tapes of anti-Chinese character, or any products or materials from Taiwan are not permitted into the People's Republic of China, nor are 'pornographic' publications or items. Occasionally, reading materials and tapes are checked by customs officials at the border, and any offensive articles are confiscated.

On arrival at Lo Wu station on the Hong Kong side of the border, the traveller will leave the train and walk across the bridge to Shum Chun on the Chinese side. As he crosses, officials of the People's Liberation Army will collect his passport and visa, and then direct him to a waiting room. When his name is called, the traveller will present his currency and customs declarations, and identify all his luggage (including that which has been checked through to Kwangchow) all of which may be fully inspected. On completion of the inspection, a further wait is necessary while fellow travellers complete the formalities.

During the wait at Shum Chun, tea, and sometimes lunch, will be served. In the lunch room, travellers will be required to sit with their respective visitor classification, e.g. businessman, diplomat, or husband and wife travelling together. Even if friends travelling together fall into separate classifications, they are expected to observe them, seating themselves separately at the indicated tables.

Eventually, the travellers will board a comfortable, air-conditioned train for the final two-hour trip to Kwangchow.

CURRENCY

In the past, U.S. currency and travellers' checks have not been welcome in the People's Republic of China, but this is now changing and any freely convertible currency can be used. The latest information on this will always be available in Hong Kong. Many businessmen recommend that travellers coming via Hong Kong take all their currency in Hong Kong dollars, but Sterling currency and travellers' checks can also be used.

All moneys and means of payment must be listed on a Bank of China form when entering China, and all conversions into Chinese currency must be made at an authorized exchange and listed on this form. It must be carefully retained until departure from China since reconversion and the export of unspent moneys will only be permitted on the basis of this form. Chinese currency may not be brought into, or taken out of, the People's Republic of China.

China's currency is the Renminbi (RMB), which means 'people's money'. Its unit is the Yuan, which is divided into ten Jiao, or into 100 Fen. Notes are issued in denominations of ¥10, ¥5, ¥2 and ¥1, as well as in 5, 2 and 1 Jiao. Coins are issued in denominations of 5, 2 and 1 Fen. Due to the comparatively low price structure in China, as well as the strict government control thereon, higher value notes have not been issued or found necessary.

Approximate foreign exchange conversions for major currencies are (as of August 1972):–
R.M.B. 5.50 per one British pound sterling;

R.M.B. 0.44 per one new French franc;
R.M.B. 0.70 per one West German Deutsch Mark;
R.M.B. 0.39 per one Hong Kong dollar;
R.M.B. 0.73 per 100 Japanese yen;
R.M.B. 2.25 per one United States dollar.

These values do fluctuate, and there is also a slight difference in rate between purchase and sale of Renminbi.

KWANGCHOW (CANTON)

On arrival in Kwangchow, foreign visitors are met by representatives of the China Travel Service with transportation to their hotels, to which their checked baggage is also brought directly from the train. Westerners are usually put into the 1,000-room Tung Fang Hotel, while Japanese are usually assigned to the new Kwangchow Hotel, and Overseas Chinese to the Renmin Hotel. These assignments do not always hold true during the trade fairs when all hotels are overcrowded, but experienced fair travellers agree that all three hotels have adequate, though not fancy, facilities and service. At the hotel, the businessman checks in at a special desk, where he is assigned to his room and also obtains his pass to the trade fair upon presentation of his invitation card.

Hotel rooms cost between ¥14 (US$6.25) for a single and ¥50 (US$22.10) for a suite, per day. Air conditioning during the hot months is turned on during the noon hours and in the evenings, and a slight extra charge is usually made. The hotels have bar-restaurants where local beer and spirits are available. They also have recreation rooms with table tennis and billiards, as well as souvenir shops, post office branches and foreign exchange banks open at certain hours of the day.

The Tung Fang Hotel restaurant serves Western, Chinese, Moslem and vegetarian cuisine at very reasonable cost, ranging from ¥2 (US$0.90) to ¥7 (US$3.10) per day. Beer and spirits are, however, more expensive. There are many excellent restaurants in the city of Kwangchow. Newcomers will probably be directed to them by their more experienced colleagues during the fair. Best known are the North Garden Restaurant, the South Garden Restaurant, the Friendship Restaurant and the Moslem Restaurant, but there are dozens of others. Reservations can be made for lunch and dinner. If a larger party is to be taken, it is advisable to book a table and order the meal well in advance, especially during the trade fair.

Foreign visitors usually take taxis to get around in Kwangchow, although a free bus service to and from the fair is provided morning, noon and evening. Taxis come in various sizes and cost. A trip from the Tung Fang Hotel to the Export Commodities Fair costs ¥1.40 to ¥2.20 (US$0.65 to US$1.00), depending on the class of taxi used. They can also be hired by the day. Except at the hotels, taxis are not always easy to obtain. It is therefore best to hold taxis until business or shopping are finished to return to the hotel, or to arrange to be picked up again at a specific time and place.

Within three days of arrival in Kwangchow or anywhere else in China, foreign visitors must register at the local Public Security Bureau. This office must also be informed of any intentions to travel to any other city, or to leave China, two days in advance of such travel, and is responsible for making any necessary visa changes while the foreigner is in the People's Republic of China. Normally, China Travel Service officials or interpreters will assist with these details, since foreign languages are not spoken in the Public Security Bureau.

During the fair periods, especially on weekends, officials of the State Trading Corporations will invite foreign businessmen to visit factories, communes or other places of interest, as well as sporting activities and performances of Chinese national opera. Excursions outside the city are also possible, although permission must be obtained. Apart from his business activities, the visitor will have much free time on his hands, especially in the evenings. Apart from the major hotels, there are no clubs or bars, Western films or television. The hotel bars do serve as a popular meeting place for visitors to get acquainted and talk, and possibly play some cards in order to while away the evenings. It is advisable to bring along to China a good supply of reading material, such as paperback books, which often are later exchanged with other foreign visitors. In Kwangchow, a small transistor radio will permit reception of news and other programs from Hong Kong.

It should be noted that scrupulous honesty and morality are customary in the People's Republic of China. Therefore, visitors must be prepared to observe mature and sober decorum during their stay. Incidences of rudeness or disrespect toward any person or toward the People's Republic, as well as any tendency to be overly affectionate or suggestive toward women can result in serious complications, including expulsion from the country, for foreign businessmen and other visitors. The story is still told to all newcomers of the Japanese fair visitor who put his arms around a waitress to thank her for her services after a lengthy, and liquid, Chinese dinner. He found himself expelled, and en route back to Hong Kong by train on the following morning.

Visitors are free to go by foot or taxi or bus to virtually any part of Kwangchow, which has many parks, museums and other points of interest. A guide, whom the hotel or China Travel Service will provide, is recommended for the latter since all signs and descriptive literature are in Chinese only. There are also numerous opportunities for shopping in department or specialty stores, or in the so-called 'Friendship Stores' which are especially for foreigners. These not only permit the visitor to purchase souvenirs or other Chinese-made products, but give another insight into the range and quality of merchandise produced in the People's Republic of China. Since all prices are fixed, there is no bargaining.

PEKING AND SHANGHAI

In some cases, a visit to the State Trading Corporation headquarters in Peking is necessary to finalize a major contract, and foreign businessmen have also been invited to visit Shanghai for additional negotiations under certain circumstances.

In this case, the State Trading Corporation concerned and the China Travel Service will arrange for the necessary visa changes, transportation, hotel and other facilities. Travel will usually be by Chinese airline, which provides regular service between the major cities. Although rail travel in China is quite comfortable, the distances involved usually preclude usage for business purposes. It takes almost 36 hours to go by train from Kwangchow to Peking, while it takes less than four hours by plane.

Foreigners visiting Peking are usually accommodated in the Peking Hotel, or the Hsin Chiao Hotel. Their restaurants serve both Western and Chinese food, and Peking also has a large number of excellent restaurants, many of which specialize in the world-famous Peking duck. This can be seen by their names, which include the Large Peking Duck Restaurant, and the Small Peking Duck Restaurant. Other popular and recommended eating places are the Minorities Restaurant and the Capital Restaurant.

A visitor to the capital should not miss the opportunity to visit the Forbidden City, the Summer Palace and, if possible, the Great Wall and the Ming Tombs outside the city of Peking. Usually, the State Trading Corporation hosting the foreign businessman will arrange for such visits. Individual arrangements can also be made through the China Travel Service, which will provide transportation and guides.

Business in Peking is done at a very leisurely pace. Days may pass between appointments or conferences, and the foreign businessman can again expect to have considerable free time on his hands.

Shanghai, the center of Western trade and business for decades prior to the political upheavals of the past thirty years, is still much more Western in its outlook and business methods today. The foreign businessman will be quite surprised at the efficiency and speed of negotiations here after having been to Kwangchow or Peking.

The Peace Hotel and the International Hotel are the two most popular for foreign visitors. Accommodation and service at both are considered better than in Peking or Kwangchow. Both hotels have good restaurants for Western and Chinese food, and there are other good restaurants in the city.

Being primarily industrial, Shanghai does not have many large parks or beauty spots within the city. However, the foreign businessman will have a chance, if interested, to visit some of the heavy industrial complexes of the People's Republic of China here. On a weekend, he can probably also arrange a visit to Hangchow and the beautiful West Lake, which are only about 100 miles from Shanghai and can be reached quite easily by train. Even in Shanghai, the once famous (or infamous) night life is no more. Cultural performances, sightseeing, shopping, reading or talking with other foreign visitors are the only leisure time activities, as is the case anywhere in the People's Republic of China.

LEAVING CHINA

Before commencing the voyage home, an exit permit from the People's Republic of China is required, and two days advance notice must be given to the local Public Security Bureau. Normally, the sponsoring trade corporation or the China Travel Bureau will handle these formalities for the foreign businessman, but they should not be overlooked. No tipping is permitted in China, but one should thank hotel employees, waitresses and others individually for the services rendered during his stay in China.

Departure formalities again include currency and customs controls. The Bank of China form on which all currency was listed at the time of entry into China, and on which all exchanges of money have been noted, must be presented at the border in order to reconvert unused Chinese currency, which may not be taken out of the country. Unprocessed photographic films (see below) and any other materials, such as Chinese books or records, which could contain state secrets or material contrary to the interests of the People's Republic of China may not be exported or taken out of the country. Antiques, including old embroidery and silks, porcelain, scrolls or other art objects may only be taken out if they meet official requirements concerning value, age and quantity. All antique shops in main cities have exportable items marked with a red seal, which must remain intact together with the purchase receipt, for inspection at the time of departure from the country.

If any commercial samples have been brought into China, these must be re-exported on departure, or must have been properly imported. In this case, the State Trading Corporation concerned will handle the details, but the import must be officially noted on the visitor's customs papers to avoid problems at the time of departure.

POSTAL SERVICES AND COMMUNICATIONS

Every major hotel will have a postal desk open during certain hours of the day, where stamps may be obtained and letters and parcels mailed.

Airmail letters to Europe or America take an average of six days, although sometimes less when a fortunate connection to one of the direct airline flights is made. Rates are similar to other international airmail rates. Surface mail for letters and parcels is also available to or via Europe by means of the Trans-Siberian railway, but takes a minimum of four to six weeks to reach its destination.

Parcels are, of course, subject to customs inspection before mailing and are subject to the same export restrictions as goods carried by the visitor when he leaves the country.

Telegrams can be sent to most destinations from the People's Republic of China. They are classified as urgent, ordinary or letter-telegrams and are charged accordingly. Except during the busiest times, an urgent telegram will reach its destination in Europe, America or Asia within two or three hours, but an ordinary telegram can take as long as twelve hours. Urgent rate telegrams cost more than US$1 per word to Europe or America, double the ordinary rate. It is recommended that businessmen planning to send many, or lengthy, telegrams from China should arrange for collect facilities to their home office. This must be done before leaving their home country, by application to the government postal authority or commercial communications carrier having contact with the Chinese administration. A card will be issued which will permit telegrams to be sent without pre-payment in China, and the costs will be billed to the home office.

Telephone traffic from the People's Republic of China has been rather limited in the past, but the purchase by China of a satellite ground station from the Radio Corporation of America, following the 1972 visit of President Nixon, is expected to improve telephone and other communications greatly in the near future. Between Kwangchow and Hong Kong, telephone and telegram service is quite speedy and efficient. During the trade fairs, many foreign businessmen arrange to keep a contact in Hong Kong with whom they are in regular telephonic or telegraphic touch for the relay of information to and from their home offices.

GENERAL INFORMATION

BUSINESS HOURS are, in general, between 8 a.m. and noon, and 2 p.m. and 6 p.m., but appointments are not normally made on Friday or Saturday afternoons. Sundays are observed as a holiday. Stores are usually open from 8 a.m. until 7 or 8 p.m. without any lunch break, and some are also open on Sundays.

Only three official holidays are observed in the People's Republic of China: (1) the Chinese (lunar) New Year or Spring Festival, which is a three-day holiday in late January or February; (2) the national Labor Day, on May 1st; (3) China's National Day, a two-day holiday on October 1st and 2nd.

CLIMATE: North China, including Peking, is extreme, averaging $22°F$ $(-7°C)$ in December-January, and over $80°F$ $(27°C)$ in July-August. Most of the year, Peking is extremely dry, windy and dusty, except during the rainy season in July and August.

South China, including Kwangchow, is sub-tropical, with an average winter temperature of about $55°F$ $(13°C)$ and a long, hot and humid summer, with temperatures averaging up to $85°F$ $(29°C)$ until late October.

Shanghai is very humid all year. Summers are similar to south China's in heat and humidity, while average winter temperatures are around $35°F$ $(2°C)$. Rainfall is heavy.

CLOTHING. Visitors to north China during winter require very warm and heavy winter clothing. Lightweight summer wear is needed in Kwangchow during fair time, when dress is quite informal and businessmen are casually dressed in shirtsleeves. Jackets are worn in the evenings, but are usually taken off while attending a Chinese dinner.

INTERPRETERS AND SECRETARIAL SERVICES: Business visitors generally negotiate in English through good interpreters provided by the State Trading

Corporations. Contracts are also usually drawn up in English, as well as Chinese. Interpreters for German, French, Spanish, Italian and Japanese are also available if advance notice of their requirement is given. Even though the Chinese negotiators may know English or other foreign languages, all business is generally handled through interpreters.

Secretarial services are not available in China. Businessmen requiring them should include a secretary in their group. The secretary should bring along a supply of stationery, carbons, stencils and other required items.

MEDICAL TREATMENT, if required while in China, is excellent, and foreign visitors receive the best possible care. Although a wide variety of Chinese medicines are available, prescriptions and instructions are in Chinese only. It is therefore recommended that visitors requiring certain regular medications bring their own supply from home when coming to China. Opiates and other habit-forming drugs are not permitted to be taken into China.

PHOTOGRAPHY AND FILMS: When entering or leaving the People's Republic of China, photographic equipment must not contain film, nor may exposed, undeveloped films be brought into or taken out of the country. On departure, undeveloped films may be confiscated, but arrangements can be made for forwarding the films to the foreigner's home after development and inspection by the Chinese authorities.

Since they have not been able to process all Kodak color films in China, they do not permit the import or use of this film. Agfa and Fuji color films, both positive and negative, are acceptable, and all brands of black and white film can be used. In China, only Chinese and East German films, which are improving in quality, can be purchased.

No difficulty is presented to visitors who wish to take pictures while sightseeing at places of historic or scenic interest. Pictures of official buildings, factories or individuals should not be taken without permission. Photography at airports and while flying over China is strictly forbidden, as are all pictures of military installations or subjects.

SOCIAL CUSTOMS: The family or surname is always placed first in China, where all names have two or three syllables. Mr Li Shih-yu should be addressed as Mr Li.

It is customary to exchange name cards, especially at business meetings, and a good supply of these should be brought along by the foreign visitor. Although not essential, it is advantageous to have one side printed in Chinese. This is best done in Hong Kong, where the proper modern simplified Chinese characters used in the People's Republic can be utilized.

Chinese dinner parties usually begin and end early by Western standards, and guests should arrive punctually, or even a little in advance of the stated time. The host normally toasts the guest of honor early in the meal, and the guest will reply with his own toast shortly thereafter. Alcoholic beverages at a Chinese meal should not be drunk until a toast has been made, and it is customary to toast other persons at the table, or even at other tables in the same party, throughout the meal. At the end of the dinner, the guest of honor makes the first move to depart. All such dinner parties are usually ended by 8.30 or 9 p.m.

TIME in China's main cities — Peking, Shanghai and Kwangchow — is eight hours ahead of Greenwich Mean Time, seven hours ahead of Central European Time, and thirteen hours ahead of Eastern Standard Time in the United States. At 8 p.m. in China, it is 1 p.m. of the same day in central Europe, and 7 a.m. of the same day in New York City.

VOLTAGE in China is usually 220 volts/50 cycle alternating current. Plugs are normally the two-pin flat American type, but many hotel rooms also have connections for the two-pin round continental European plugs. It is recommended that conversion plugs for razors or other appliances be taken along.

VII. CONTRACTS AND AGREEMENTS

FOREIGN TRADE ORGANIZATION AND LIABILITY

The Ministry of Foreign Trade is the Chinese Government organization which negotiates foreign trade agreements, regulates the issuing of licenses for foreign trade, and controls the Customs Office and the Administration for the Inspection and Testing of Commodities. Since the various foreign trade organizations are directly under the control of the Ministry of Foreign Trade there is the legal problem of the possibility of the trading organizations pleading sovereign immunity as a defense to court action. Furthermore, the liability of these corporations is limited to the working capital appropriated to them by the State and, like all other State enterprises, this is controlled by the Chinese People's Bank of the State Council. Since they are only middlemen in a planned economy, these corporations would have limited capital.

To make matters even more complicated for the Western corporation's lawyers, the People's Republic of China has not enacted a Commercial Code. In none of China's contracts is there any specific reference to the legal system under which the contract is written. For example, the wheat sales which were concluded with Australia and Canada do not specify an ultimate legal body, although in the case of the Canadian sales, provisions have been made for arbitration in Switzerland. When contracts are concluded between the China Resources Company in Hong Kong as representative of the Chinese, it is difficult to ascertain to what degree that company is responsible and to what degree the Chinese Government would allow it to be held liable in the event of claims. Legally speaking, the China Resources Company of Hong Kong, which acts as agent for nine of the PRC foreign trade organizations, is a firm composed of eleven Chinese partners. When the company makes a contract with a foreign buyer or seller it does so without mentioning the fact that it is acting as an agent. It is questionable, therefore, whether it should be legally considered as an agent without personal liability or as buying and selling on its own account just as an import and export firm would.

If it is any consolation for the businessman worried about his legal position *vis-a-vis* trade with China, the Bank of China could be considered to be a separate juristic person in the legal sense even though it is controlled and directed by the Chinese People's Bank. It is a joint state/private enterprise where private investors are given a fixed five per cent dividend per year and enjoy various voting rights. As a separate juristic person the defense of sovereign immunity in legal cases would not be available to it.

STANDARD FORM CONTRACTS

The Chinese trading corporations rely on their own form contracts for buying and selling in common transactions. These form contracts give maximum protection to the Chinese side. While the terms of the purchase contracts bind the foreign seller very tightly, the selling contracts are quite loose. Most traders have accepted these conditions because of competition for China trade and also because the Chinese have been liberal in their interpretations of contracts. They have very seldom exacted penalties from suppliers in default. However, although they have been careful to meet their contracts for supply, in 1958 and 1959 they were unable to make deliveries against a wide range of contracts for agricultural products.

The languages normally used in contracts are English and Chinese. Very often in contracts with English-speaking countries, only English is used. However, there are cases where both English and Chinese versions are given and considered to be equally authentic. Thus there is the possibility of deadlock over interpretation in cases of conflict.

PAYMENT

Except in the event of credit terms, the Chinese normally follow the procedure of opening a letter of credit with the Bank of China in favor of the seller 15 to 20 days prior to delivery date. This credit is payable against the presentation of the opening bank's draft and the shipping documents. The letter of credit is normally valid until 15 days after the shipment is effected. When they are purchasing, the Chinese normally specify in great detail the documents required before payment is to be made. These documents most often include a bill of lading, commercial invoices, packing lists and the manufacturer's quality and quantity weight certificates. Since the Chinese often open their letter of credit within China in a branch of the Bank of China, the foreign seller is therefore without either the goods or the documents for a short period.

In the case of purchases from the Chinese, they most often specify payment against sight draft drawn under a confirmed, irrevocable, divisible and assignable letter of credit without recourse for the full amount, established through a bank acceptable to them. The Chinese also often request buyers not to specify in the letter of credit any particular shipping line, steamer name or insurance company. They ask that letters of credit be stipulated so as to remain valid for at least ten days after the last day of shipment and with a plus or minus five per cent allowance of the credit and quantities. Letters of credit must reach the Chinese at least fifteen days before the month of shipment stipulated in the confirmation, unless otherwise stated.

SHIPMENT

When exporting, the Chinese want the freedom to ship from any Chinese port with the date of the bill of lading taken as the date of shipment. Changes in destination not agreed upon beforehand are not allowed. If such changes are made, the extra freight or insurance costs are charged to the buyer. Since the Chinese try to ship as much as possible on their own vessels, deliveries are not always on time. When purchasing, the Chinese most often import on FOB (Freight on Board) and C&F (Cost and Freight) terms. They do not allow CIF shipments since they assume insurance themselves. If the shipment is FOB, Sinofracht Chartering and Shipbroking Corporation in Peking will handle shipping arrangements. In the case of FOB terms, contracts most often specify that thirty days prior to shipment date, the seller must notify the Chinese buyers of the day the goods will be at the port of shipment, in addition to all details regarding quantity, value, number of packages, gross weight and contract number. Ten days before arrival of the vessel designated by Sinofracht Peking or their agents, a notice is sent to the sellers to arrange shipment. If the vessel does not arrive at the loading port within 30 days after the arrival date given by the Chinese, they agree to bear storage and insurance expenses from the 31st day. If the shipment is not ready for loading after the carrying vessel has arrived at the port of shipment, the sellers are liable for any dead freight and demurrage. After the goods have passed over the vessel's rail and released from the tackle, all risks and expenses are undertaken by the Chinese buyers.

In the case of C&F terms, the Chinese most often do not allow trans-shipment. If the goods are sent by parcel post or air freight, the sellers must notify the Chinese buyers 30 days before the time of delivery or the estimated delivery date and supply all identifying information. After the despatch of the goods the sellers must advise the Chinese buyers of the name of the vessel, date of sailing, identifying information and date of despatch.

PACKING AND LABELLING

The Chinese will normally manufacture only under their own labels even in cases where they manufacture to the specifications of the buyer. However, if the buyer wants to have his own trademark, label, stamping or method of folding or packing, this should be agreed upon at the initial negotiations.

Exports to China should be marked for the 'People's Republic of China' or 'China' but definitely not 'Red China', 'Communist China' or 'Mainland China'.

Packing must be able to withstand, besides the long sea journey, exposure and open-air storage on arrival in the Chinese port of destination. The Chinese buyers are quite particular about packing, and damage claims for faulty packing are often made. Wooden boxes are preferred to cartons. Individual boxes should not be too heavy since mechanical loading equipment is not always available in China.

SPECIFICATIONS, GUARANTEES AND CLAIMS

When purchasing from China it is important that buyers clearly state all details regarding specifications. For example, if 'Made in China' is desired in the English language, this should be so stated. Packaging should be clearly specified. Tolerances plus or minus three per cent to five per cent are allowed for measurements and/or weight. Form contracts usually state that the Chinese suppliers will not be responsible for details of designs, styles, sizes, colors and other factors not reaching them at least 45 days prior to the month of shipment stipulated in the confirmed order.

When they are buying, the Chinese buyers ask that the sellers guarantee that the item being purchased be made of the best materials with first-class workmanship, and is new and unused. The form contracts normally allow a period of 90 days after arrival of the goods for the Chinese to make claims. The contracts will usually stipulate that in the case of claims, failure to answer the claim within one month is an assumption of acceptance.

TESTING AND INSPECTION

The Chinese standard form contracts for both the purchase and sale of goods specify the Commodity Inspection and Testing Bureau as the final arbiter in the case of disputes. Although Western lawyers may not find this arrangement satisfactory, the Bureau has established for itself a good reputation for fairness among foreign traders and there are stories of how goods destined for export from China were rejected for export by the Bureau as not reaching minimum standards.

The Bureau is part of the Ministry of Foreign Trade and has more than fifty branches at China's main production, distribution and transportation centers. It issues certificates of origin, certificates of inspection and testing, survey reports for weight, and notary certificates certifying various facts such as whether delivery has actually been made, etc.

ARBITRATION

The form contracts used by the Chinese for buying and selling normally specify that all arbitration will be undertaken before the Foreign Trade Arbitration Commission of the China Council for the Promotion of International Trade in Peking, rather than to an international arbitration body. However, in a number of cases, such as in large wheat sales, the contracts have provided for arbitration outside China. It must be emphasized, in any case, that the Chinese prefer negotiation in an informal manner to a legalistic approach to arbitration. This is a natural consequence of Chinese traditions where emphasis is on friendly long discussions rather than formal negotiations.

TRADE MARKS, PATENT PROTECTION AND ROYALTIES

Trade marks may be registered in China by arrangement with the China Council for the Promotion of International Trade. However, patents may not be registered and sellers of patented equipment or other items must be prepared to release this know-how in any sales to China, since the Chinese will not respect patent laws established in various parts of the world. Sales of technical know-how are possible, but the Chinese most often insist on lump sum payments.

VIII. THE FUTURE

Opinions about trade possibilities with the People's Republic of China are mixed. On the one hand we look at China's 700 to 800 million people living on a vast land mass and are overwhelmed. On the other hand there are the pessimists who say that China trade has never, and will never, amount to much. These pessimists point to the Government-controlled structure of the Chinese trading firms, the apparently small list of items which China has to sell and the comparatively low level of present trade. Regrettably, these differences of opinion are symptomatic of a short-range approach to the study of world trade. It underscores the need for a reconsideration of past and present approaches and realities.

China has not, up to this time, been a big factor in world trade. During the twenty-two year period from 1950 to 1971 China's total trade, including imports and exports, never exceeded US$4.6 billion dollars. By comparison, Taiwan, whose population and land mass is miniscule in relation to the People's Republic of China, had total trade in 1971 amounting to US$4.2 billion dollars.

China has exhibited a practical and pragmatic approach to world trade with politics often taking a back seat to hard trade facts and realities. The cycle from predominant trade with non-Communist countries to a predominance of Communist country trade and back again to a predominance of Free World trade, has been completed during the last twenty years. In 1954 and 1955, 74 per cent of China's trade was with Communist countries. By 1970 that portion had decreased to 20 per cent. Coincidentally, it seems that the country trade pattern existing before World War II is again emerging. Before the War, Great Britain, Japan, the United States, Hong Kong, France and Germany were the leading trading partners. Now all of those countries except the U.S. are major trade partners of China.

If we are to find meaning in China's trade situation, we must keep a number of key characteristics of China's economy in mind. First, the history of China's trade with the rest of the world, although extending far back in time, did not really reach a substantial scale until the 1840s.

Second, China's industrialization is a relatively new phenomenon. Modern industry in China did not start until the 1890s when the Ch'ing government established several arsenals. Soon after that the first cotton mills appeared. Then, when foreigners were permitted to operate factories in the treaty ports, modern industry began on a significant scale.

Third, China's industrialization, despite the Chinese efforts at self-reliance, has been heavily dependent on foreign trade inputs for its development. We have just mentioned the foreign factories in the treaty ports. These factories provided the base for foreign investment. In 1911, of the US$120 million investments in industries, only about 20 per cent was domestic capital. In 1939 of the US$8.5 million of capital investment in China, 42 per cent was foreign owned. During the 1931 to 1944 period Japanese investment in Manchuria resulted in industrialization there. Foreign investment, of course, did not only mean the investment of equipment and money but the dissemination of ideas, skills, techniques and managerial expertise.

The fourth key characteristic is that China's trade and industrialization has exhibited an ability to rise suddenly to unprecedented high rates of growth and absorb capital inputs of enormous proportions. For example, the industrialization drive in the 1952 to 1957 period, although followed by the 'Great Leap Forward' failure, could probably be ranked as one of the greatest efforts in world history in terms of industrial output increases, new capital formation, material utilized and number of people involved. Another indication of the absorption capacity of the Chinese economy can be seen by the scale of Russian inputs between 1950 and 1960. Initially, the plan called for the Russians to aid in construction and reconstruction of 156 major industrial enterprises including seven iron and steel plants, 24 electric power stations and 63 machinery plants. About 130 of those projects were completed, involving imports of about US$3 billion worth of equipment and machinery from Russia.

Finally, the leaders of the People's Republic of China have proved their ability and determination to push their nation rapidly toward industrialization and economic strength. To what degree this leadership will want to utilize foreign trade to bolster the industrialization and development drive remains to be seen. Self-reliance has been the keynote of economic policy in recent years. However, Chen Ming, Minister of Foreign Trade once said: "In our time no country can develop its economy in isolation. The more an economy develops, the more foreign trade is needed. This is true of both capitalist and socialist countries."